Practice Tests Plus

B1 Preliminary

NEW EDITION

Helen Chilton • Mark Little • Helen Tiliouine

with Michael Black and Russell Whitehead

Pearson Education Limited
KAO Two,
KAO Park,
Harlow,
Essex.
CM17 9SR
and Associated Companies throughout the world

www.english.com/practicetestsplus

First published 2019
6th Impression 2024
ISBN 978-1-292-28215-2
Set in Helvetica Neue LT 10/12pt and Gill Sans 10/12pt
Printed in Great Britain by Ashford Colour Press Ltd.

We are grateful to the following for permission to reproduce copyright material:
Illustration Acknowledgements
John Batten (Beehive Illustration Ltd) 29, 30, 31, 53, 54, 71, 72, 88, 107, 108, 125, 126, 143, 161, 200, 201, 202, 203, 204, 205, 206, 207; **Nigel Dobbyn** (Beehive Illustration Ltd) 30, 31, 53, 54, 71, 72, 88, 89, 107, 108, 125, 126, 144, 161, 162.

Photo Acknowledgements
The publisher would like to thank the following for their kind permission to reproduce their photographs:
123RF.com: 62, 116, 140, designpics 44, erwinova 123, kadettmann 11, maridav 193, olegdudko 80, robinsphoto 116, sam74100 134, stockbroker 98, szefei 116; **Alamy Stock Photo:** Cultura Creative (RF) 44, Fabio Camandona 196, robertharding 69, Visuals Stock 116; **Getty Images:** James Woodson 192; **Pearson Education Ltd:** Gareth Boden 62, 62, 116, 192, Joey Chan 197, Jon Barlow 11, 62, Jörg Carstensen 98, Jules Selmes 98, 158; **Shutterstock.com:** 122, 141, 194, 195, 198, 663268 11, AJR_photo 134, 152, Alberto Zornetta 134, Blend Images 98, Bukhta Yurii 87, Dragon Images 134, Ebtikar 152, @erics 44, Flashon Studio 11, HeinSchlebusch 11, Hugo Felix 80, Ijansempoi 80, India Picture 44, Ikoimages 159, Michaelpuche 199, nenetus 198, nortongo 86, Olena Hromova 22, otnaydur 62, Pavel L Photo and Video 197, Peter Polak 152, polkadot_photo 98, Rawpixel.com 20, 134, sirtravelalot 194, SnowWhiteimages 80, Stuart Monk 195, Syda Productions 196, trabantos 138, trattieritratti 104, v.s.anandhakrishna 80, vgstudio 152, WAYHOME studio 152, wildestanimal 68, William Perugini 44, 193, 199, Yakobchuk Viacheslav 105, Zheltyshev 102

All other images © Pearson Education

PRACTICE TESTS PLUS NEW EDITION RESOURCES

Where to find and how to use

Access on the **Pearson English Portal**:

	Resource	Description	When to use
AUDIO	Test 1 Training activities Tests 1–8	Audio files for Listening tests and Training.	Throughout the book.
	Audioscripts	Full scripts for the Training activities and Tests 1–8.	During or after completing any of the activities or tests as extra support.
WRITING	Sample answers	Three sample student answers for each piece of writing: – email – article – story	When Test 1 training is complete, use with Test 2 Writing. Sample student answers are written using Test 2 questions, the worksheets aim to help students write good answers to these questions.
	Examiner feedback for each sample answer	Examiner feedback on the three sample student answers for each piece of writing: – email – article – story	
	Student activity worksheet by writing genre	Worksheet 1 – email Worksheet 2 – article Worksheet 3 – story Page 1 – focuses on sample answers and examiner feedback on these to help students understand what makes a 'good' answer. Page 2 – builds process writing skills and gives additional language input.	
SPEAKING	Videos	Speaking test About the exam Candidate feedback Frequently asked questions Examiner feedback	Watch with or without the worksheets described below.
	Student activity Worksheets	Worksheet 1 – focus on test format Worksheet 2 – focus on Part 1 Worksheet 3 – focus on Part 2 Worksheet 4 – focus on Part 3 Worksheet 5 – focus on Part 4 Page 1 – focuses on real students' answers and what makes a good response. Page 2 – focuses on building confidence and useful language for the test.	Worksheet 1 – use with *About the exam* video Worksheet 2 – use with *Speaking test video Part 1* Worksheet 3 – use with *Speaking test video Part 2* Worksheet 4 – use with *Speaking test video Part 3* Worksheet 5 – use with *Speaking test video Part 4*
	Video transcripts	Speaking test About the exam Candidates' feedback Frequently asked questions Examiner feedback	During or after watching any of the videos as extra support.
VOCABULARY MAPS	Vocabulary maps for over 20 topics	Vocabulary items organised by topic to help students extend their vocabulary.	Find the matching topic and use with any test to build vocabulary.

Access on the **Pearson English App**:

	Resource	Description	When to use
AUDIO	Test 1 Training activities Tests 1–8	Audio files for Listening tests and Training activities.	Throughout the book.
SPEAKING	Videos	Speaking test About the exam Candidate feedback Frequently asked questions Examiner feedback	Watch with or without the speaking test worksheets.
VOCABULARY BUILDING PRACTICE	Topic-based vocabulary practice	Each topic includes a practice exercise on meaning and one on use.	Find the matching topic and use with any test to build vocabulary.

EXAM OVERVIEW

The *Cambridge Preliminary English Test*, also known as **PET**, is made up of **four papers**, each testing a different area of ability in English. The Reading, Writing, Listening and Speaking papers each carry 25% of the marks. There are five grades: A, B and C are pass grades, D and E are fail grades. Candidates also receive a numerical score on the Cambridge Scale for each of the four skills.

Reading   45 minutes
Writing   45 minutes
Listening   30 minutes (approximately)
Speaking   12 minutes (approximately) for each pair of students.

Paper	Format	Task Focus
Reading 6 tasks, 32 questions	Part 1: 5 short texts, multiple choice, 5 questions, 3 options each.	Understanding short messages of different types.
	Part 2: Match 5 descriptions of people with 8 short texts.	Reading for specific information and detailed comprehension.
	Part 3: Longer text, multiple choice, 5 questions, 4 options.	Reading for gist, global and detailed meaning, attitude, opinions and feelings.
	Part 4: Gapped text, choose correct sentences to put in gaps, 5 gaps, 8 options.	Reading to understand gist and text structure.
	Part 5: Gap fill text, choose missing words, 6 questions, 4 options.	Reading for specific meaning (vocabulary).
	Part 6: Open gap fill, write words in the gaps, 6 questions.	Reading for specific meaning (grammar).
Writing 3 tasks, 2 questions	Part 1: Write an email in response to information given (about 100 words).	Focus on writing a short informative text using appropriate language.
	Part 2: Write either an article or a story on the topic given (about 100 words).	Focus on writing a short creative or factual text using appropriate language.
Listening 4 tasks, 25 questions	Part 1: Multiple choice, 7 short recordings, 3 picture options.	Listening for specific information.
	Part 2: Multiple choice, 6 short recordings, 3 options.	Listening for attitudes and opinions.
	Part 3: Gap fill. Write 1 or 2 words in 6 gaps in a short text about the recording.	Listening for specific information.
	Part 4: Multiple choice, 6 questions, 3 options.	Listening for specific information, detailed meaning, attitudes and opinions.
Speaking 4 tasks	Part 1: Introductory phase, examiner-led conversation.	Candidates show ability to use general interactional and social language.
	Part 2: Individual long turn. Visual prompts.	Describing photographs and managing discourse, using appropriate vocabulary in a longer turn.
	Part 3: Collaborative task. Visual prompts.	Using functional language to make and respond to suggestions, discuss alternatives, make recommendations and negotiate agreement.
	Part 4: Discussion with another candidate.	Talking about likes/dislikes, preferences, habits, opinions and agreeing/disagreeing. Linked to collaborative task in Part 3.

CONTENTS

Practice Test 1   **6**
with Training activities

Reading   6
Writing   23
Listening   28
Speaking   38

Practice Test 2   **42**
with Tip strips

Reading   42
Writing   52
Listening   53
Speaking   58

Practice Test 3   **60**

Reading   60
Writing   70
Listening   71
Speaking   76

Practice Test 4   **78**

Reading   78
Writing   88
Listening   89
Speaking   94

Practice Test 5   **96**

Reading   96
Writing   106
Listening   107
Speaking   112

Practice Test 6   **114**

Reading   114
Writing   124
Listening   125
Speaking   130

Practice Test 7   **132**

Reading   132
Writing   142
Listening   143
Speaking   148

Practice Test 8   **150**

Reading   150
Writing   160
Listening   161
Speaking   166

Grammar bank   **168**

Speaking bank   **182**

Writing bank   **186**

Visuals for Speaking tests   **192**

Part 2 Candidate A   192
Part 2 Candidate B   196
Part 3   200

General questions   **208**

OVERVIEW
TEST 1: READING

About the paper

There are six parts. You read both short and long texts and answer different types of questions. In Parts 1–3, you have to show that you can read and completely understand the texts. In Parts 4–6, you have to both read the texts and show that you can use language correctly.

The test lasts 45 minutes. This includes the time you spend writing your answers on the separate answer sheet.

For Parts 1–6, there is one mark for each correct answer.

How to do the paper

Part 1

In Part 1, you read five short texts on different topics. Some of the texts are notices you might see in different places. Others might be messages, such as emails, phone messages, etc. There is one multiple-choice question about each text. Each multiple-choice question has three options (**A**, **B** and **C**). You have to choose the option which is closest to the meaning of the text.

Part 2

In Part 2, you read eight short texts. They are all on the same topic and contain similar ideas and information. For example, you could read eight reviews of websites or information about eight different courses or places. You also have to read information about five people. You have to decide which person matches each short text. For example, you might need to decide which website each person would find most useful or which course they should do.

Part 3

In Part 3, you read one longer text. This might be about a person, an event or something else. You have to answer five multiple-choice questions about the text. Each multiple-choice question has four options (**A**, **B**, **C** and **D**). The questions are about details in the text, as well as about feelings, attitudes and opinions expressed by the writer or a person in the text.

Part 4

In Part 4, you read one long text about an interesting person, place or event. This time, five sentences are missing from the text. After the text, there is a list of eight sentences (**A–H**). You have to choose the five missing sentences and decide which one fits each gap. In this way, you show that you can use reference words like pronouns and other vocabulary to link together the ideas in a text.

Part 5

In Part 5, you read one short text. Six words are missing from the text. For each missing word, there is a multiple-choice question, which gives you four possible words to use in the gap. You have to choose the best word (**A**, **B**, **C** or **D**). You look at the words before and after the gap to help you choose the best one. In this way, you show your understanding of vocabulary and how words are used together in a text.

Part 6

In Part 6, you read one short text. Six words are missing from the text. You have to think of the missing word yourself to fill each gap. In this part, the missing words are mostly grammatical words like pronouns, prepositions, etc. By writing the correct word, you show that you understand how to use grammatical words to write good sentences.

PART 1: TRAINING

Focus on the instructions

1 Look at the exam task on pages 8 and 9.

  a How many questions do you have to answer?

  b What do you have to decide?

  c How many options do you have to choose from for each question?

2 Look at this example below. What kind of text is it?

  a a notice   **b** an email   **c** a note

> Charlie,
> Please can you get my coat from the dry cleaner's when you pick up your suit? I'll give you the money this afternoon if that's OK.
> Thanks a lot!
> Vera

3 Where might you see it?

4 What does the note say?

  a Vera will pay Charlie back for the dry cleaning later.

  b Charlie should take his clothes to the dry cleaner's.

  c Vera's suit needs to be collected from the dry cleaner's.

5 Look at the correct answer to question **4** above. In the note, underline the words which have a similar meaning to *pay back* and *later*.

6 Why is option **b** in question **4** wrong? Is Charlie taking clothes to the dry cleaner's or picking them up?

7 Why is option **c** in question **4** wrong? What belongs to Vera at the dry cleaner's? What belongs to Charlie at the dry cleaner's?

Focus on the questions

1 Look at question **1** on page 8. What kind of text is it?

  a a sign   **b** a note   **c** a label

2 Now answer these questions about question **1**.

  a Where might you see it?

  b What might you do before you see it?

  c Underline the words in option **A**, **B** or **C** which have a similar meaning to *while your books are checked*.

3 Now look at question **2**. What kind of text is it?

  a a note   **b** a postcard   **c** an email

4 Now answer these questions about question **2**.

  a When might you receive this kind of text?

  b Underline the words in the text which you think are positive things to say.

  c Underline the words in the text which you think are negative things to say.

  d Does the word *disadvantage* in the question relate to positive or negative things?

5 Look at question **3**. What do you think is the relationship between Sandra, Betty and Paula?

6 Answer these questions about question **3**.

  a Which of these sentences from the text is about what Sandra needs to do?

    i *Paula's emailed twice about the guest list for the party.*

    ii *Could you send it to her as soon as you can?*

  b What does *it* refer to in *Could you send it to her as soon as you can?*

7 Look at question **4**. Where might you see a text like this?

8 Now answer these questions about question **4**.

  a Look at option **A**. What do you usually get in a canteen? Does the text say that you can get an ID card in the canteen?

  b Look at option **B**. Is it correct? Why?

  c Option **C** is wrong. What does the text say about staff?

9 Look at question **5**. What kind of text is it?

  a an email   **b** a text message   **c** a label

10 Answer these questions about question **5**.

  a When is the training usually?

  b Who booked the training for this week?

  c What time are they going to train this week?

Part 1

Questions 1 – 5

For each question, choose the correct answer.

1

> **RIVER SCHOOL LIBRARY**
>
> Wait in this area while your books are checked.
>
> Thank you.

A   You must tell us if you leave books here for checking.

B   Check that you have all your books before leaving the library.

C   Do not leave here until we have checked your books.

2

> Countryside here's OK. Mountains higher than we expected. Very limited wildlife, though the other people in the group are fun and we have easy transport.
>
> Deshini

In Deshini's opinion, what is the countryside's disadvantage?

A   the transport

B   the animals

C   the mountains

3

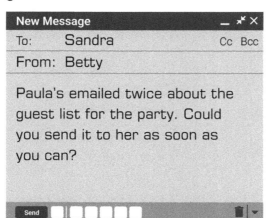

> **New Message**   — ⤢ ✕
>
> To: Sandra   Cc Bcc
>
> From: Betty
>
> Paula's emailed twice about the guest list for the party. Could you send it to her as soon as you can?
>
> Send

What does Sandra need to do?

A   Let Paula know who's going to the party.

B   Send a party invitation to Paula.

C   Ask Paula who should be invited to the party.

4

SOUTHWOOD COLLEGE CANTEEN

Staff and students cannot use the canteen without ID cards.

A   Students can get their ID cards in the canteen.

B   Staff must bring their ID cards if they want to use the canteen.

C   Students need to show staff their ID cards.

5

< Back   Contacts

The football coach rang. Nobody from our team has booked to come at 2, only other teams. This week, to be together, we'll have to train at 4 instead.

A   We need to change the training time because it's full at 2 p.m. this week.

B   We may have to train with a different team this week.

C   We must go training at a later time this week.

PART 2: TRAINING

Focus on the instructions

1 Look at the task on page 11.

a How many questions do you need to answer?

b How many options are there to choose from for each question?

c What do all the people want?

d What are the advertisements for?

e What do you need to decide?

Focus on the questions

1 Read text **6** on page 11 and answer these questions.

a What does Omar want to find out about?

b Who does he want to meet?

c What does he want to see?

d Underline the three parts of the text that gave you the answers to questions **a–c**.

2 Now read text **7** and answer these questions.

a What is Cecile's favourite thing to do?

b What does she want to make better?

c Why does she want to meet other people?

d Underline the three parts of the text that gave you the answers to questions **a–c**.

3 Read text **8** and answer these questions.

a Where does Duncan like going?

b How does he travel?

c What does he want to learn about?

d Underline the three parts of the text that gave you the answers to questions **a–c**.

4 Read text **9** and answer these questions.

a What does Heidi like doing?

b Can she always do this?

c What does she want to know about?

d Underline the three parts of the text that gave you the answers to questions **a–c**.

5 Read text **10** and answer these questions.

a What does Piotr study?

b What do you think Piotr likes more, IT and business or modern art?

c Can he always go to galleries and museums?

d Underline the three parts of the text that gave you the answers to questions **a–c**.

6 Look at these words about Omar's interest in text **6**: *architecture*, *building*. Find and underline words like these in advertisements **A–H**.

7 Look at advertisements **A–H** again. Answer these questions.

a In which advert have you underlined more words than others?

b Does this text contain information about the three things that Omar wants?

c Which advertisement should you choose for question **6**?

8 Look at the important information you underlined in texts **7–10**.

- Then read through advertisements **A–H** again.

- Underline words in the advertisements which have a similar meaning to the information you underlined in texts **7–10**.

9 Now decide which advertisement contains the correct information for each person **7–10**. Why are these answers not correct?

a 8 C

b 9 E

c 10 F

Questions 6 – 10

For each question, choose the correct answer.

The people below are all looking for a magazine to buy.

On page 12 there are eight advertisements for magazines.

Decide which magazine would be the most suitable for the people below.

6  Omar is interested in architecture and wants to know more about it. He would like to meet people with the same interest and to visit special buildings locally.

7  Cecile is very keen on sport and keeping fit, and particularly enjoys long-distance running. She would like to improve her technique and perhaps find other people to run with.

8  Duncan enjoys spending his free time in the countryside, exploring different areas on foot and by bike. He wants to know more about what he sees when he is exploring.

9  Heidi likes going to watch her favourite football team, although she usually has to work at weekends, organising jazz concerts. She's keen to learn about the history of football.

10  Piotr is studying IT and business at university, but he's very interested in modern art, although he's usually too busy to visit galleries and museums.

This month's pick of the magazines

A   World of Sport

This is *the* magazine for sports fans! All team sports are covered, with reports on games (in case you miss any), interviews with players and much more. There are lots of photos and special articles on subjects such as the early beginnings of football and baseball clubs in distant places.

B   History is Beautiful

Art and music lovers will really enjoy this magazine. It's full of interesting articles about the history of concert music, classical architecture around the world and the development of the great museums and galleries.

C   Footloose

Are you someone who loves being outside, looking after your body? *Footloose* is the magazine for the outdoor runner who takes their hobby seriously. Professional advice is given, with tips for achieving the best style on long runs. There are also lists of local clubs you can contact or join.

D   Green World

The busier our city lives become, the more we want to escape to the fields and hills. *Green World* is the magazine to take with you. There's lots of information about birds, animals, trees and plants, together with maps of great bike rides and walks to follow.

E   Sport Business

Interested in sport? Want a career in sport? Want to study sport? This is the magazine for you! Maybe you want to learn about setting up a health club or a bike shop, or about how football clubs operate in the business world. It's all in here.

F   Plan for Success

This magazine is all about setting up businesses that will succeed in today's difficult economic climate. With articles about motivation from famous sportspeople and tips for running companies without waste, you can learn all you need to get ahead.

G   How We Live

Houses, offices, museums, bridges … Somebody designed them, somebody built them – but most people walk straight past them. Learn about the structures we live and work in. *How We Live* also contains a list of local associations, so you can share your enthusiasm with like-minded people nearby.

H   Pictures in Your Living Room

This is the magazine for today's art lover. Every month there are large high-quality reproductions of famous pictures from the twentieth and twenty-first centuries. Turn your home into an exhibition hall of these masterworks, building up a great collection.

Focus on the instructions

1 Look at the exam task on pages 14–15.

    a What do you have to read?

    b What do you have to do?

    c How many questions are there?

    d How many options are there for each question?

2 Read the text quickly and answer these questions.

    a What activity is the writer mainly talking about?

    b What did the writer think about camping when he was a child?

    c Where did the writer go camping when he was a child?

    d Does the writer think campsites are the best places to stay in?

    e Who does the writer go camping with these days?

Focus on the questions

1 Read questions **11–15** on page 15. Choose the correct words to complete these statements. The information in brackets will help you.

    a Question **11** asks about *the writer's friends / the writer*.

    (This is always a question about detail, attitude, feeling or opinion.)

    b Question **12** refers to *where the writer used to live / what the writer used to feel*.

    (This is always a question about detail, attitude, feeling or opinion.)

    c Question **13** asks about *opinion / detail*.

    (This is always a question about detail, attitude, feeling or opinion.)

    d Question **14** is about *the future / the past*.

    (This is always a question about detail, attitude, feeling or opinion.)

    e Question **15** asks about what the writer *has said / is likely to say*.

    (This is always a question which asks about information from several different parts of the text.)

2 Look at these sentences from the text. Put them in the order in which they appear in the text.

    a *I think every family should have that opportunity.*

    b *Although many campsites have great showers and shops, and are usually good value for money, they're also quite boring places to be.*

    c *My father worked in the music industry and my family moved from city to city.*

    d *We could see they loved it: the freedom, cooking on a fire, looking at the stars at night.*

    e *But of course, the opposite was also sometimes true.*

3 Now read question **11** again and look at options **A–D**.

    A Does the writer tell us that some of his friends had never tried camping?

    B Does the writer show us that his friends had very different opinions about camping?

    C Does the writer suggest that some people had more to say than others?

    D Does the writer say that some of his friends didn't want to talk about camping?

4 In question **12** the correct answer is **D**. Can you underline the part of the text that includes this information?

5 In question **13** the correct answer is **A**. Can you underline the part of the text that includes this information?

6 In question **14** the correct answer is **A**. What are the 'simple things' in the text?

7 In question **15** the correct answer is **C**. Can you underline the parts of the text that contain this information? Why are options **A**, **B** and **D** wrong?

Part 3

For each question, choose the correct answer.

___

Camping

Journalist Gary Timms writes about his love of camping.

When I asked a group of my friends whether they enjoyed camping, everybody had plenty to say. Camping was either terrible or wonderful – there was rarely anything in between. Their opinions depended on their childhood experiences. If they'd had fun staying in tents in the countryside when they were kids, then that was usually the beginning of a life-long love of camping. But of course, the opposite was also sometimes true.

Personally, I loved camping when I was younger and I believe that's why I still do today. My father worked in the music industry and my family moved from city to city. I was sometimes rather lonely, I realise now, though I wasn't unhappy. During the holidays, I visited many different places and saw all sorts of interesting tourist sights with my family. We often stayed in nice hotels, but for me, real holidays were the ones when we got out into the countryside and slept in tents. I think every family should have that opportunity.

The kind of camping I liked best was 'wild camping': not stuck in campsites, but up in the mountains, in forests or by rivers. After all, if you're camping with friends or family, that's who you want to be with, not a load of strangers. Although many campsites have great showers and shops, and are usually good value for money, they're also quite boring places to be. However, a night at a campsite once in a while allows you to get all your clothes clean and stock up with food. And wherever you choose to camp, don't pack too many things: keep it basic and you'll have a better time.

We took our three children camping last summer. We could see they loved it: the freedom, cooking on a fire, looking at the stars at night. I like to think that they understood the value of fresh air and water, sunshine, running and swimming, and that it meant more to them than an expensive holiday touring countries on the other side of the world.

11 What did the writer discover when he asked his friends about camping?

    A   Some of them had never been able to try it.

    B   They had very different views on the subject.

    C   The ones who liked it had the most to say.

    D   A few of them preferred not to discuss the topic.

12 What does the writer say about his childhood?

    A   He wished his father would spend more time at home.

    B   He frequently felt rather miserable.

    C   He was glad his family could afford luxury accommodation.

    D   He enjoyed one type of holiday more than any other.

13 What does the writer say about campsites?

    A   It's useful to stay in them occasionally.

    B   Most of them are rather expensive.

    C   They rarely have enough facilities.

    D   They're a good place to meet new people.

14 The writer hopes that on their camping holiday his children learnt

    A   the importance of simple things.

    B   how to manage money carefully.

    C   the names of the stars they saw.

    D   how to cook new dishes.

15 What would the writer say to someone who wants to try camping?

    A   If you go camping, make sure you take a good map with you that shows where to find the best campsites.

    B   It's probably best to wait until your children are older before you take them on a camping trip.

    C   You must definitely try camping with your kids, and the less you take with you, the more you'll enjoy the experience.

    D   Remember that camping can be quite dangerous, so plan your trip very carefully and don't go too far away from other people.

PART 4: TRAINING

Focus on the instructions

1 Look at the exam task on pages 17–18.
  a What do you have to read?
  b What do you have to do?
  c How many gaps are there?
  d How many sentences are there?
  e Do you have to use all the sentences?

2 Read the text quickly. What is it about?

3 Match the four paragraphs of the text with these headings.
  a Looking for the *Mary Rose*
  b Ordinary people learning about the *Mary Rose*
  c Reasons why the *Mary Rose* ended up at the bottom of the sea
  d Objects the sailors took on board the *Mary Rose*

Focus on the questions

1 Read the text again carefully and decide which of the sentences **A–H** should fill each gap.

2 Now answer these questions
  a In question **16**, the correct answer is **H**.
    i What does *However* mean: 'but' or 'also'?
    ii What does *them* in sentence **H** refer to? Underline the words in the sentence before the gap.
  b In question **17**, the correct answer is **F**.
    i What does *as a result* mean: 'actually' or 'because of that'?
    ii What does *As a result* in sentence **F** refer to? Underline the words in the sentence before the gap.

  c In question **18**, the answer is **A**.
    i Underline the words in the sentence before the gap which refer to finding the *Mary Rose*.
    ii What does *They* in sentence **A** refer to? Underline the words in the text before the gap.
  d In question **19** the answer is **G**.
    i What does *these* refer to? Underline the words in the sentence before the gap.
    ii Look at the sentence after the gap. Underline the pronoun which 'these' in sentence **G** refers to.
  e In question **20**, the answer is **D**.
    i What does *so* mean: 'for this reason' or 'for example'?
    ii What does *they* in sentence **D** refer to? Underline the words in the sentence before the gap.

Focus on the language

1 Read these sentences and think about the connection between them. Choose the correct option to complete them.
  a The children were hungry after the journey and wanted to eat as soon as they arrived. *Because / So* it was lucky that their grandma had cooked a big meal for *her / them*.
  b The café where he was writing his essay was very noisy. *That's why / That's how* he went to the library to write it *also / instead*.
  c My family gave me a camera for my birthday. *It / They* took me out for dinner *too / now*.

  d They don't need to get up early tomorrow. *For example / After all*, they're *on holiday / at work*.
  e There were a lot of interesting places to see on the island. *However / Finally*, many of *these / theirs* were difficult to reach by car.
  f There are lots of useful *jobs / projects* that you could do when you're older. *For instance / As a result*, you could become a nurse or a firefighter.

Part 4

Questions 16 – 20

Five sentences have been removed from the text below.

For each question, choose the correct answer.

There are three extra sentences which you do not need to use.

The *Mary Rose*

The *Mary Rose* was a sixteenth-century sailing ship used by King Henry VIII of England to fight wars. The ship sank in July 1545 during a battle off the south coast of England, near the city of Portsmouth. Soon afterwards, a number of attempts were made to raise the *Mary Rose*. **16** [   ] The ship became half buried in sand and clay, and lay at the bottom of the sea for more than 400 years.

During that time, the *Mary Rose* was occasionally disturbed. For example, during the nineteenth century, two divers brought up a few objects from the sunken ship. But over the following 100 years, the ship became completely covered up and disappeared under the bottom of the sea. **17** [   ] Then, in 1965, a team of volunteer divers started to search for the ship, exploring the area using sonar technology. In May 1971, three large pieces of wood from the ship were discovered. **18** [   ] In 1982, after many years of hard work, most of the ship was brought up out of the sea.

The *Mary Rose* had a large crew. When the ship was found again, thousands of items like clothes and cooking equipment belonging to them were discovered inside it. **19** [   ] After the ship was raised, experts were delighted to be able to study them. The crew had also needed to entertain themselves during their free time. **20** [   ] All this gave historians useful information about what daily life was like in the sixteenth century.

Naturally, the general public were also very interested, and followed the story of the *Mary Rose* closely as it was reported in newspapers and on TV. Now, at a museum in Portsmouth, visitors can see the remains of the ship and many of the objects it was carrying when it sank.

A   They had finally found the *Mary Rose*!

B   For instance, nobody expected that there would be so much in them.

C   After all, there was no reason for anyone to keep on looking.

D   So they had taken games and musical instruments with them, too.

E   This is why they wanted to explain what had happened to it.

F   As a result, the exact location of the *Mary Rose* was forgotten.

G   Fortunately, many of these were still in excellent condition.

H   However, none of them were successful.

PART 5: TRAINING

Focus on the instructions

1 Look at the exam task on page 20.

   a What do you have to read?

   b How many questions are there?

   c What do you have to choose?

   d How many options do you have to choose from for each question?

2 Read the text on page 20 and answer these questions.

   a Is it factual or is it a story?

   b Is it difficult to understand what the text is about?

   c Are there any questions about the meaning of the text?

   d Is it a long text or a short text?

Focus on the questions

1 Now look at question **21**.

   a Which two verbs are used to introduce 'some people's' opinions?

   b Look at the sentence after the gap. Notice that there is no word like 'if' or 'whether' there. Which of the two verbs is correct?

2 Look at question **22**. Which of the possible answers can we use with 'work'?

3 In question **23**, which of the options means 'stay in a place'?

4 Look at question **24**. Notice the word *as* after the gap. Which of the options is the only verb that can be followed by an object + 'as'?

5 In question **25**, which of the options means 'good in this particular situation'?

6 Look at question **26**. Notice *a break* after the gap. Which of the options completes this idiomatic phrase correctly?

Focus on the language

1 Look at the options **A–D** for questions **21–26** again. Now choose one of the options from each question to complete the sentences below.

   a I .... if that's a good idea. (Question **21**)

   b That doesn't .... to be a good idea. (Question **21**)

   c I'm looking for our exact .... on this map. (Question **22**)

   d This is the highest .... of the mountain. (Question **22**)

   e The photography exhibition will .... until 16 September. (Question **23**)

   f If we .... on walking so quickly, we'll be there soon. (Question **23**)

   g How about .... a shelf out of this piece of wood? (Question **24**)

   h I'm thinking of .... these flowers in a vase. (Question **24**)

   i Do you know the .... answer to this question? (Question **25**)

   j All the runners wanted to finish the 25 km race, but not all of them were .... (Question **25**)

   k We're really tired. Can you .... us a break now, please? (Question **26**)

   l The break will .... at noon and end at 12:45. (Question **26**)

Part 5

Questions 21 – 26

For each question, choose the correct answer.

Working from home

Most people with jobs have to spend some of the day travelling. Some people may

(21) .... this is a waste of time, but not everyone can afford to live near their

(22) .... of work. And some people choose to live outside the city centre or

(23) .... in the neighbourhood where they grew up.

However, nowadays more and more people are choosing not to travel to work every

day. They work from home instead, **(24)** .... a space in their home as their

office, connected to their company by the internet. They prefer this way of working

because they feel they can do more and feel less tired at the end of the day.

If you want to do this too, make sure you have a **(25)** .... space to work in,

with good light and a comfortable chair. And remember to **(26)** .... regular

breaks!

21	A	seem	B	wonder	C	think	D	look
22	A	position	B	location	C	point	D	place
23	A	remain	B	keep	C	continue	D	rest
24	A	making	B	doing	C	using	D	putting
25	A	correct	B	suitable	C	right	D	successful
26	A	begin	B	take	C	follow	D	give

PART 6: TRAINING

Focus on the instructions

1 Look at the exam task on page 22.

   a What do you have to read?

   b How many questions are there?

   c What do you have to do?

   d How many words can you choose for each gap?

2 Read the text on page 22 and answer these questions.

   a What kind of text is it?

   b Is it difficult to understand what the text is about?

   c Are there any questions about the meaning of the text?

   d Is it a long text or a short text?

   e What kind of words are missing?

Focus on the questions

1 Look at question **27**. What kind of word is missing in each case? Answer these questions to help you decide.

   a What type of word can go between *as* .... *as* ?

   b What is the phrase *as* .... *as* about here: comparing things, time or something else?

   c What word can you put in the gap so that *as* .... *as* means 'immediately'?

2 Look at question **28**. Answer these questions.

   a What does the word *As* mean in this sentence?

   b Who is Dani writing to?

   c Who does the pronoun *I* refer to?

   d Which pronoun should be used to refer to Fran?

3 In question **29**, which word comes before *is* or *are* to say that something exists?

4 Look at question **30**. Answer these questions.

   a Read the complete sentence. Did Dani like the café?

   b Did Dani want to stay a short time or a long time?

   c Can you think of a two-word time expression with 'day' that would fit here?

5 Look at question **31**. Answer these questions.

   a How many parts does the sentence have?

   b Are the ideas in the two parts similar or different?

   c What word can you write in the gap to connect these two ideas?

6 Look at question **32**. What preposition goes before *work* to make a phrase that means 'in the place where I work'?

Focus on the language

1 Look at some more examples of the type of words that are often tested in Part 6. Complete each sentence with one word in each gap. Remember to look at the words before and after the gaps carefully.

   a This box is .... heavy for me to carry – I can't even pick it up!

   b That mountain is .... high that it's very difficult to climb.

   c I haven't seen Liz .... March, when she moved to Manchester.

   d *Highlight* is the .... interesting book I've ever read.

   e I hate travelling .... train but my sister loves it.

   f He couldn't decide whether to stay at home .... go out with his friends.

   g This sweater doesn't cost as .... as that one.

   h My cousin invited his family to the party as .... as all his friends.

   i The people .... live next door are very friendly.

   j .... I enjoyed most about the film was the music.

Part 6

Questions 27 – 32

For each question, write the correct answer.

Write **one** word for each gap.

Hi Fran,

I've just been to a great new café in the town centre, called Café K. I liked it as

(27) .... as I went in because they were playing some really good jazz. As

(28) .... know, I love that kind of music!

(29) .... are lots of plants and the whole place is very light and bright. The

staff are really friendly, too, and the coffee I had was absolutely wonderful. It was

so nice that I wanted to stay **(30)** .... day! It wasn't too busy when I went,

(31) .... I'm sure it will become very popular when more people find out

about it.

So, when will you be free to come and visit Café K with me? I'm **(32)** .... work

tomorrow and the day after, but maybe we could meet on Thursday.

All the best,

Dani

About the paper

There are two parts in the Writing test and you must write two pieces. The first is always an email (Part 1). The second is a story or an article (Part 2). In Part 2 you choose which type of text you want to write.

You have 45 minutes to do the Writing test, so you have 20–25 minutes for each part. This includes the time to read the tasks and think about them before you start writing, and the time to decide which task to choose in Part 2.

You get the same number of marks in Part 1 and in Part 2, so you must try to do both well. The examiner will give you good marks if:

• you have included all the information

• your writing is clear and easy to follow and understand

• you have used some good language, with good spelling and punctuation.

How to do the paper

Part 1
In Part 1, there is only one task, which you must do. On the page you will see an email from a friend, a teacher or another English-speaking person, with four notes around it. Your task is to write an **email** replying to this person, using all the notes. You should write about 100 words.

Part 2
In Part 2, there is a choice between two tasks: a **story** or an **article**. You must choose one of them and write about 100 words. For the story, you are given the first sentence, which is the beginning of the story. For the article, you are given the title and also some questions that you must answer.

How do I decide what to choose in Part 2?
Don't waste too much time deciding. Choose the one you like most! Look at the two tasks. Think about these things.

• Do I like the topic of the article?

• Do I understand what I need to write about?

• Can I think of some ideas to make the article interesting?

• Do I know some interesting vocabulary I can use?

• Do I like the way the story begins?

• Do I have some good ideas to make my story interesting?

• Do I know some interesting vocabulary I can use?

See **WRITING BANK** for sample answers, useful language and practice

See **GRAMMAR BANK** for reference and practice

PART 1: TRAINING

Focus on the instructions

1 Read the instructions on page 25 and answer these questions.

   a Do you have to do this question or can you choose to do a different one?

   b What are you going to write?

   c Who are you going to write to?

   d How many things do you need to write about?

   e How many words do you need to write?

Focus on the questions

1 When planning your answer, it is useful to ask yourself these questions. Read question **1** on page 25 and answer these questions.

   a Why are you writing?

   b Who are you writing to?

   c Do you know this person?

2 Read the notes around the email again. What information do they tell you to include? Choose the correct answer **a** or **b**.

Great!

   a Respond positively to Anna's congratulations.

   b Congratulate Anna.

Explain

   a Say whether you like the mountains or the city.

   b State your choice of subject: the mountains or the city.

Tell Anna

   a Name a person who can go with you.

   b Name a person you like.

Ask about …

   a Give Anna further information she needs.

   b Tell Anna what information you need.

3 Look at your answers for exercise **2**. Write a sentence for each correct answer.

Focus on the language

1 Read a student's answer to question **1**. Choose the correct answer **A**, **B** or **C** to complete it.

	A	**B**	**C**
1	For	Dear	So
2	can't	wouldn't	mustn't
3	What	How	This
4	where	the	which
5	there	if	because
6	like	as	with
7	little	a	one
8	when	to	about

New Message

(1) .... Anna,

Thank you for your email. I **(2)** .... believe I actually won the competition! **(3)** .... a brilliant prize, thank you!

It's hard to choose **(4)** .... best place to go because they are both interesting, but I think I'd like to go to the city **(5)** .... I'd love to learn to take better pictures of people and buildings. My best friend and my brother are keen photographers **(6)** .... me, so I'll invite them to come with me.

There's just **(7)** .... thing I'm wondering about: when can I go on this holiday? Is there a particular date or can I decide?

I look forward **(8)** .... hearing from you.

Best wishes,

Mark

Part 1

You **must** answer this question.

Write your answer in about **100 words**.

Question 1

Read this email from Anna Jones, the organiser of a photography competition, and the notes you have made.

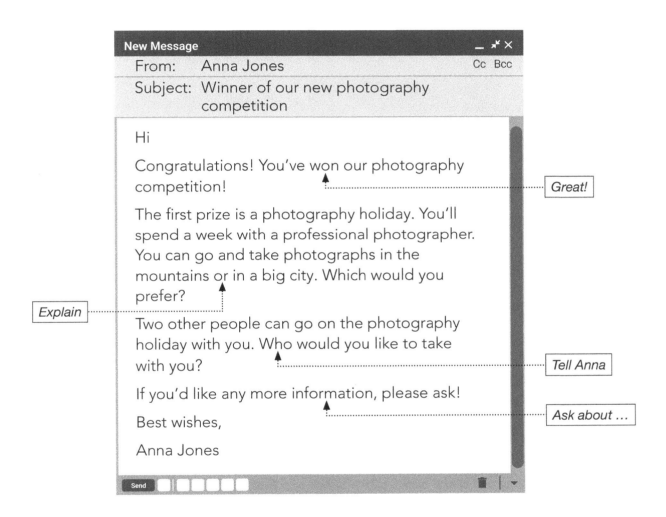

New Message   _ ⤢ ×

From: Anna Jones   Cc Bcc

Subject: Winner of our new photography competition

Hi

Congratulations! You've won our photography competition! .... **Great!**

The first prize is a photography holiday. You'll spend a week with a professional photographer. You can go and take photographs in the mountains or in a big city. Which would you prefer?

Explain ......

Two other people can go on the photography holiday with you. Who would you like to take with you? .... **Tell Anna**

If you'd like any more information, please ask! .... **Ask about ...**

Best wishes,

Anna Jones

Send

Write your **email** to Anna using **all the notes**.

PART 2: TRAINING

Focus on the instructions

1 Look at the exam task on page 27.

a How many questions are there in this part of the exam?

b How many questions do you have to answer?

c How many words should you write?

Focus on the questions

1 Read question **2** on page 27 and follow these steps to help plan your answer.

- Write down three ideas for your article.
- Write down five useful words or phrases that you could use in your article.

2 Now read question **3** and follow these steps.

- Look at the sentence given and think of a story you could write. What happens in the second sentence? How will the story end?
- Write down five useful words or phrases that you could use in your story.

3 Look at your notes for exercises 1 and 2 above and choose which question you will answer. Think about these things.

- Do you have enough ideas for the article? Do you know all the vocabulary you'll need? Can you write 100 words?
- Do you have enough ideas for the story? Do you know all the vocabulary you'll need? Can you write 100 words?
- Which of the questions seems easier to you?

4 Read a student's answer to question **2**. Complete it with the words and phrases from the box.

| a group of   an easy way   it's great   keen on |
| make me   nothing better than   without |

I enjoy watching many different kinds of films. I like comedies because they **(a)** .... laugh and thrillers because they're really exciting. I'm also **(b)** .... historical films which teach me something about the period they're set in. It's **(c)** .... to learn about the past **(d)** .... reading history books!

I think **(e)** .... to be able to lie on the sofa in my living room, watching one of my favourite films for the twentieth time. However, for me, there's **(f)** .... sitting in front of a giant screen at the cinema with **(g)** .... friends, laughing or being scared together!

Focus on the language

1 Read a student's answer to question **3**. Complete it with the phrases in the box.

| across the room   banging noise |
| been here for   fell over   had forgotten |
| had left   there was |

I was glad when my phone started to ring. I'd waited all morning for her call and I was starting to think Gina **(a)** .... all about me. I ran **(b)** .... to answer it, but my brother **(c)** .... so many things on the floor – clothes, books, a football – that I **(d)** .... ! When I

finally got to my phone, it had stopped ringing and there was no number on the screen. Was it Gina? What should I do? Then I realised I could hear a **(e)** .... .Was there someone at the front door? I went downstairs to check. I opened the door and **(f)** .... Gina! 'Your doorbell doesn't work,' she said. 'I've **(g)** .... ages! Why didn't you answer your phone?'

Choose **one** of these questions.

Write your answer in about **100 words**.

_____

Question 2

You see this announcement on an English-language website.

Articles wanted!
Films

What kinds of film do you like? Why?

Do you prefer watching films at the cinema or at home?

We'll publish the best articles on our website next month!

Write your **article**.

Question 3

Your English teacher has asked you to write a story.

Your story must begin with this sentence:

I was glad when my phone started to ring.

Write your **story**.

OVERVIEW
TEST 1: LISTENING

About the paper

There are four parts. You listen to long and short recordings and answer different types of questions. In Parts 1 and 2, you hear short recordings and answer one question about each recording. In Parts 3 and 4, you hear one long recording and answer six questions in each part. You hear each recording twice.

The test lasts approximately 35 minutes. You are given time at the beginning of each part to read the questions. You also have 6 minutes after you have heard all the recordings to transfer your answers to the separate answer sheet.

For Parts 1–4, there is one mark for each correct answer.

How to do the paper

Part 1

In Part 1, there are seven different recordings and a question to answer about each one. In some recordings, you hear one person, for example someone leaving a phone message. In others, you hear two people talking about something in an everyday situation. For each question, there are three pictures (**A**, **B** and **C**). You listen to the question and decide which picture shows the best answer. The questions are mostly about information like times, prices, what people like best or what people decide to do. Listen carefully because the recording mentions the things in all three pictures, but only one picture correctly answers the question.

Part 2

In Part 2, there are six different recordings and they are all conversations between two people. There is one question about each recording, but this time the answers are multiple-choice. You hear a sentence that tells you who is speaking and what they are talking about. Then you have time to read the question and three options (**A**, **B** and **C**). You listen and choose the best option. You need to listen for things like the speakers' attitudes, opinions and feelings. You don't usually hear the same words that you read in the options, so think about the meaning of what the people are saying. Some questions ask about one of the people, but others ask about what the people agree or what they both say. Always listen carefully to what each person says.

Part 3

In Part 3, there is one long recording and there is always just one person talking. For example, you may hear someone giving a presentation or someone making an announcement. You hear a sentence that tells you who is speaking and what they are talking about. You then have time to read a set of notes or sentences from which some of the information is missing. Read this carefully and think about the information you need to fill each of the six gaps. When you listen, follow the information in the task and be ready to write the missing information in the gaps. Write the exact word(s) or number(s) you hear. Always listen carefully. You may hear some of the words that are written in the task or words that mean the same thing. You may also hear more than one word that could fit in a gap – think carefully about the word you need. Sometimes the recording gives the spelling of a word, like somebody's name, for example. Listen to the letters carefully.

Part 4

In Part 4, there is one long recording, which is always an interview. You hear a sentence that tells you who is being interviewed and what the topic is. For example, it could be a sportsperson or a celebrity, or someone who has done something interesting. You then have time to read six multiple-choice questions. Each one refers to one of the questions that the interviewer asks in the recording. You listen and choose which option (**A**, **B** or **C**) answers each question. Remember that the questions come in the same order as the information in the recording. Listen carefully and think about the meaning of what the person says. You don't usually hear the same words that are written in the questions or options, but you do hear the person talking about the ideas.

PART 1: TRAINING

Focus on the instructions

1 🔊 Listen to the introduction to the test and answer these questions.

   a How many parts does the listening test have?

   b How many times will you be able to listen to each part?

   c When can you ask questions?

2 Read the instructions and look at the task on pages 30–31. Answer these questions.

   a How many questions are there?

   b How many pictures are there for each question?

   c What do you have to do?

3 Look at this example question and the three pictures.

   • What is the same in the three pictures?

   • What is different in the three pictures?

   Which are Sara's cousins?

4 🔊 Listen to the recording for the example question in exercise 3. Answer these questions.

   a What colour hair have Sara's cousins got?

   b What are they wearing?

   c Which picture shows two boys like this?

Focus on the questions

1 Look at the questions on page 31. What are the times shown on the three clocks in question **1**? Can you think of more than one way of saying each time?

2 Now look at question **2**. What can you see in each picture?

3 Look at question **3**. Practise telling somebody how to go from the house to the school by each route, **A**, **B** and **C**.

4 What are the different objects in the pictures in question **4**?

5 What can you see in each picture in question **5**?

6 What is happening in each picture in question **6**?

7 What are these things used for in each picture in question **7**?

8 Look at these extracts from the recordings for questions **1–7**. Complete them with the words in the box.

> along behind couple fallen farm
> have like never only plates till wild

   1 OK, but the film isn't .... half past, is it?

2 I think the elephant is the one to go for because it's another .... animal, while the horse is more of a .... animal, maybe.

3 I turn right when I come out of my house, and then go on till I .... to go left, and then school's just ahead, ... the road.

4 Sure – a .... of cartons?

5 But I realised when I took my towel out that I .... put my toothbrush in, ... the toothpaste – which is pretty useless now!

6 A tree has .... across the street and there are lorries that can't pass, so now all the cars are stuck .... them and can't move at all.

7 Well, I turned it on so that I could wash the .... , but now water's coming out of it – .... out of the shower!

9 🔊 Listen and check your answers.

10 Now try the exam task.

Part 1

Questions 1 – 7

For each question, choose the correct answer.

___

1   What time does the film start?

   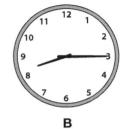   

    A   **B**   **C**

2   Which picture does the boy want?

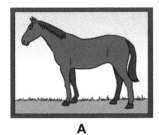      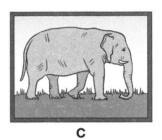

    A   **B**   **C**

3   How does Valentina get from her house to school?

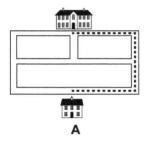   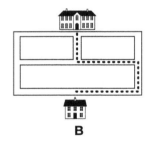   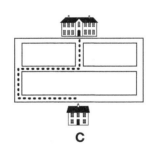

    A   **B**   **C**

4   What does Sally need?

    A   **B**   **C**

5 What did the man forget to pack?

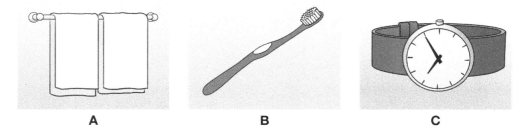

A   B   C

6 What problem is there in the town?

A   B   C

7 What needs to be repaired?

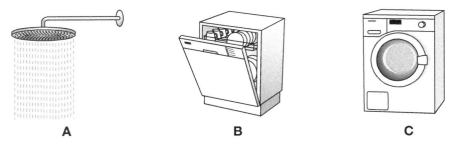

A   B   C

PART 2: TRAINING

Focus on the instructions

1 Look at the exam task on page 33.

  a How many questions are there?

  b What do you need to do?

  c How many options are there to choose from for each question?

Focus on the questions

1 🔊 Read question **8** on page 33 and listen to the recording. Answer these questions.

  a Who says the characters are unusual – the woman, the man, both or neither of them?

  b Who says the ending is sad – the woman, the man, both or neither of them?

  c Who says the story is exciting – the woman, the man, both or neither of them?

  d What is the correct answer?

2 🔊 Now listen to the recording again and answer these questions about it.

  a Do you hear the words *sad*, *exciting* or *unusual* in the recording?

  b What do the speakers say that helps you to choose the correct answer?

3 Now look at question **9**. What do you think are some good and bad things the woman might say about these subjects?

  a the food

  b the weather

  c the accommodation

4 🔊 Listen to the recording for question **9**. Answer these questions.

  a What does the woman say about the things in question **3** above? Were you right?

  b What does she not like?

  c Now choose the correct answer **A**, **B** or **C**.

5 🔊 Look at question **10**. The correct answer here is **A**. Now listen to the recording for question **10**. What two things do the speakers say which mean their boss *explains things clearly*?

6 🔊 Now look at question **11** and listen to the recording. Answer these questions.

  a In what order does the man talk about these things: a) price, b) size, c) design? Is it the same order as these things appear in options **A**, **B** and **C**?

  b What does the man say is small: the table or the kitchen?

  c Does he think the table is a bit expensive or too expensive?

  d What does the man say about the style of their flat? Does he think that's a problem?

  e What is the correct answer?

7 🔊 Look at question **12** and listen to the recording. Answer these questions.

  a What does the man say about his performance? Does that match option **B**?

  b What does he say about the other musicians? Does that match option **C**?

  c What does he say about the audience? Does that match option **A**?

8 🔊 Finally look at question **13** and listen to the recording. Answer these questions.

  a Why did the girl go to the library?

  b What did she realise when she went home?

  c What is the correct answer?

For each question, choose the correct answer.

---

8   You will hear two friends talking about a film.
       What do they agree about it?

   A   The ending is sad.

   B   The story is exciting.

   C   The characters are unusual.

9   You will hear a woman telling a friend about a holiday.
       What did she dislike about it?

   A   the food

   B   the weather

   C   the accommodation

10   You will hear two colleagues talking about their boss.
        Why do they like her?

   A   She explains things clearly.

   B   She has a good sense of humour.

   C   She listens when staff have personal problems.

11   You will hear a couple talking about a table.
        What does the man say about it?

   A   It's too expensive.

   B   It's too small.

   C   It's too modern.

12   You will hear a man telling a friend about playing in a concert.
        How does he feel about it?

   A   grateful to the audience

   B   satisfied with his performance

   C   positive about the other musicians

13   You will hear two college students talking about a geography project.
        What is the girl doing?

   A   giving some advice

   B   admitting a mistake

   C   confirming an arrangement

PART 3: TRAINING

Focus on the instructions

1 🔊 Read and listen to the instructions on page 35.

   a What do you need to do?

   b What can you write in each gap?

   c How much time do you have to look at the questions?

   d Who will you listen to?

   e What will this person be talking about?

Focus on the questions

1 Read the task on page 35. Think about the kind of information you will need to write in each gap.

   a In question **14** should you write a subject or a year?

   b In question **15** do you have to write an adjective or a noun?

   c What might go in the gap in question **16**, a number or a noun?

   d What should you write in question **17**, a name or a noun?

   e What is likely to go in the gap in question **18**?

   f What might go in the gap in question **19**?

2 Look at the exam task on page 35. Which word from the box below should go in each gap?

> hostel   medicine   wildlife   transport   train
> politics   spanish   dancing   fish   toilets
> bicycle   caravan

3 🔊 Listen and check your answers.

Focus on the language

1 Choose the correct words to complete these extracts from the recording in exercise 2.

   a This trip will be of particular interest to those of you *studying / learning* politics, though if there are any spare places, other people can go too.

   b She'll also discuss plans to *increase / improve* transport, which is one of her own areas of responsibility.

   c Then you'll join in an activity that'll teach you about medicine in the *period / time* when much of the castle was built, the Middle Ages.

   d He'll talk to us about various *ideas / projects* for protecting wildlife, and show us some of the improvements over the last few years.

   e We'll travel by coach to Swindon, and take the train from there to Cardiff – the whole journey will take *over / around* two hours.

   f And we'll *spend / book* three nights in a hostel.

2 🔊 Listen again and check your answers.

Part 3

Questions 14 – 19

For each question, write the correct answer in the gap. Write **one** or **two words** or a **number** or a **date** or a **time**.

You will hear a tutor talking to a group of college students about a trip.

College Trip to Cardiff

Mainly for students of **(14)** ....

First day: visit to Welsh Assembly

- Tour of the building

- Talk by a government minister about the Assembly and improvements to **(15)** ....

Second day

- Morning: tour of Cardiff Castle and chance to learn about **(16)** .... in the Middle Ages

- Afternoon: talk by member of City Council about the protection of **(17)** ....

Practical information

- Dates: 22–25 June

- Travel: by coach to Swindon and then by **(18)** .... to Cardiff

- Accommodation: in a **(19)** ....

PART 4: TRAINING

Focus on the instructions

1 🔊 Read and listen to the instructions on page 37.

a What do you need to do?

b How many questions are there?

c How much time do you have to look at the questions?

d Who will you hear?

e What will these people talk about?

Focus on the questions

1 🔊 Listen to the recording and choose the question **i** or **ii** that the interviewer asks Ronald each time.

a Question **20**
  i Did you walk a long way every day?
  ii How far did you go each day?

b Question **21**
  i Did you have to prepare?
  ii Did you need to prepare?

c Question **22**
  i Was there any particular reason for starting there?
  ii Did you have a particular reason that you started there?

d Question **23**
  i And where did you sleep?
  ii And where did you go to sleep?

e Question **24**
  i What did you enjoy most about the walk?
  ii What was the best thing about the walk?

f Question **25**
  i What did you plan?
  ii And what's that?

2 🔊 Look at questions **20–25** on page 37 and listen to the recording again. Answer these questions.

a Question **20**
  i When did Ronald walk 11 miles?
  ii When did he walk 18 miles?

b Question **21**
  i Did he need to walk up hills or mountains?
  ii When did he go on a long walk?

c Question **22**
  i Where was the sun when he started walking each day?
  ii When did the weather improve?

d Question **23**
  i When did he stay in a guest house?
  ii How often did he stay at a campsite?

e Question **24**
  i Did he like the scenery?
  ii What did he think about the animals?

f Question **25**
  i What does he say about his holiday?
  ii Did he intend to plan a talk?

Focus on the language

1 Complete these extracts from the recording with the words in the box.

along	before	else	every	helps	mostly
myself	night	put	then	thought	

a .... it was around thirteen miles.

b I took fitness classes nearly .... day, and did a long walk a week .... I started the coast-to-coast walk, to make sure I was ready for it.

c The wind generally comes from behind you, so it .... you – sometimes it was so strong it blew me .... !

d I took a tent with me and spent a .... in a campsite, though I generally .... it up close to the path, wherever I was walking.

e I suppose the best thing was having some time to .... , with no one .... around.

f I intended to plan the talk while I was walking, but .... I had the idea of writing a book about walking in Scotland, and I .... about that most of the time instead.

2 🔊 Listen and check your answers.

Questions 20 – 25

For each question, choose the correct answer.

You will hear a radio interview with a man called Ronald Ferguson, who has just walked across Scotland from coast to coast.

20 How far did Ronald usually walk each day?

    A   about 11 miles

    B   about 13 miles

    C   about 18 miles

21 How did Ronald prepare for the walk?

    A   He climbed several mountains.

    B   He went walking every weekend.

    C   He went to fitness classes.

22 Ronald started in Oban because

    A   the wind made walking easier.

    B   the sun was usually behind him.

    C   the weather was better than in the east.

23 Where did Ronald usually sleep?

    A   in guesthouses

    B   beside the path

    C   in a campsite

24 What did Ronald enjoy most about the walk?

    A   the scenery

    B   watching animals

    C   being alone

25 During the walk Ronald planned

    A   a book.

    B   a holiday.

    C   a talk.

OVERVIEW
TEST 1: SPEAKING

About the paper

The Speaking paper lasts approximately 12 minutes and there are four parts. Parts 1 and 2 take 2–3 minutes each. Parts 3 and 4 take 6 minutes in total. You take the test with a partner. There are two examiners. One examiner acts as interlocutor and speaks to you and the other just listens. In some parts you talk to the examiner and in other parts you talk to each other.

The examiner who listens marks you all through the test. You get marks for the grammar and vocabulary you use, how you organise what you say, your pronunciation, and the way you interact with your partner and with the examiner. The interlocutor also gives you a global mark. The speaking mark is 25 percent of your total score for the test.

How to do the paper

Part 1

In Part 1, the examiner asks each of you questions about yourselves. You speak to the examiner in this part, and not to each other. The first few questions are simple ones, for example, your name, where you live and what you do. You just give short, simple answers to these questions.

After this, the examiner asks you each one or two more personal questions, for example, about your likes and dislikes or your daily routines. You should give longer answers to these questions. Try to think of something interesting to say and keep talking until the examiner says, 'Thank you.'

Part 2

In Part 2, you also speak to the examiner, but there are no questions to answer. In this part, the examiner gives each of you a photograph of an everyday situation to talk about. Your photograph will show people at home or at work, or maybe doing an outdoor activity. You should say what you can see in the photograph and describe all the details; for example, where the people are, what they are doing, what they are wearing, how they are feeling. Keep talking until the examiner says, 'Thank you.' You should try to organise what you say. For example, begin by describing the people and what they are doing, before moving on to talk about the things in the background.

Part 3

In Part 3, the examiner describes a situation to you and gives you a picture with some ideas to discuss with your partner. The examiner doesn't ask you questions; instead, you have to speak to your partner. You should exchange ideas and opinions, using the ideas on the picture to help you. Listen carefully to the situation the examiner describes to you and the question you need to discuss. Look at the ideas on the picture. Try to talk about all the ideas before you come to a decision and say why each one is a good or bad idea. You have to keep talking for 2–3 minutes until the examiner says, 'Thank you'. Remember to ask your partner questions and respond to your partner's ideas, because you get marks for interacting well with each other.

Part 4

In Part 4, the examiner asks you and your partner some more questions that are connected to the topic of your discussion in Part 3. You should give your own opinion and say why you think that. Listen to your partner's questions and what your partner says because you may be asked if you agree or to give your own opinion about the same question.

See **SPEAKING BANK** for useful language and practice
See **GRAMMAR BANK** for reference and practice

PARTS 1–4: TRAINING

Focus on Part 1

1 Answer these questions from Phase 1.

1 What's your name?

2 Where do you come from?

3 Do you work or are you a student?

4 What do you study?

2 Match the examiner's questions **1–4** with the possible students' answers **A–D**.

1 Where did you go for your last holiday?

2 Do you think English will be useful to you in the future?

3 Tell me about your bedroom.

4 How do you travel to work every day?

A Usually by bus, but sometimes a colleague gives me a lift.

B Well, it's not very big. There's a bed, a desk and a wardrobe and all my things, like my guitar and my computer.

C I went skiing in the mountains in the east of my country – it was great!

D Well, I hope so! Yes, I want to work for an international company and I think my English will be essential.

Focus on Part 2

1 Look at photograph 1A on page 192 and read a student's description of it. Choose the correct words to complete the description.

This is an interesting picture. I can **(1)** *look / see* four people in it, two boys and two girls. They look quite young – I'd say they're about fifteen – and they **(2)** *would / could* be friends or classmates. They're out walking near the coast – I can see the sea in the **(3)** *foreground / background*. I'm not sure what they're doing **(4)** *exactly / possibly* – maybe they're hiking **(5)** *because / so* one of them has got a map and they've all got backpacks. The weather is sunny and it **(6)** *looks like / looks* summer because there are some flowers in the grass. Also the people aren't wearing jackets, so it **(7)** *is going to / must* be warm. They **(8)** *seem / sound* to be watching something, just **(9)** *far from / outside* the photo. I can't see what it is but you can **(10)** *tell / know* because they're all looking to the right.

Focus on Part 3

1 Read the examiner's instructions for Part 3 on page 41 and look at the pictures on page 200. Match the expressions from a Part 3 discussion **(1–5)** with their functions **(A–E)** below.

1 We could give him a nice painting like this.

2 Do you mean for the living room?

3 Maybe something like that would be too expensive though.

4 Do you think it's a good idea having a barbecue in an apartment?

5 That sounds good.

A making a suggestion

B disagreeing with a suggestion

C checking understanding

D asking for your partner's opinion

E agreeing with a suggestion

Focus on Part 4

1 Read the examiner's questions and two student's answers for each one. Which is the best answer in each case, **A** or **B**? Why?

a **Int:** Do you usually prefer to do indoor or outdoor activities in your free time?

   A: I definitely prefer being outdoors because I spend a lot of time in classes during the week. I often go jogging with my friends at the weekend, and I love horse-riding.

   B: You do activities like football, rugby and cycling outside but basketball, badminton and judo inside.

b **Int:** Do you enjoy taking part in competitions?

   A: Not really – I never seem to win anything! So I don't enjoy them much. My sister loves them though.

   B: No, not at all. I hate them.

c **Int:** Do you think it's better to have lots of different hobbies or be very good at just one?

   A: That's a difficult question – I think I'm quite good at playing the guitar.

   B: If you have lots of different hobbies then maybe you won't become very good at any of them. I think you should try different hobbies to find out what you're good at, then choose that one.

Part 1 (2–3 minutes)

Phase 1

In Phase 1 of Part 1, the examiner asks you and your partner questions about yourselves. This is what the examiner says.

Good morning/afternoon/evening.
Can I have your mark sheets, please?

I'm … and this is …
- What's your name?
- Where do you live/come from?
- Do you work or are you a student?
- What do you study?

> **Back-up prompts**
> These are some further questions the examiner may ask:
> *Do you have a job?*
> *Do you study?*
> *What job do you do?*
> *What subject do you study?*

Phase 2

In Phase 2 of Part 1, the examiner asks you each a few questions about your likes and dislikes and daily routines. For example, the examiner may ask you questions like:
- What did you do yesterday?
- Tell us about your family.
- Where do you like going on holiday?
- What did you do on your last birthday?

> **Back-up prompts**
> These are some further questions the examiner may ask:
> *Did you do anything special yesterday? What was it?*
> *Who is in your family?*
> *Where do you usually go on holiday?*
> *Did you have a party on your last birthday?*

Part 2 (2–3 minutes)

1A Spending time together

In Part 2, the examiner asks you each to describe a photograph. This is what the examiner says.

Now, I'd like each of you to talk on your own about something. I'm going to give each of you a photograph and I'd like you to talk about it.

A, here is your photograph. It shows **friends spending an afternoon together**.
[*Turn to photograph 1A on page 192.*]
B, you just listen.
A, please tell us what you can see in the photograph.

🕐 about 1 minute

Thank you.

1B Having a meal together

B, here is your photograph. It shows **a family eating a meal.**
[*Turn to photograph 1B on page 196.*]
A, you just listen.
B, please tell us what you can see in the photograph.

🕐 about 1 minute

Thank you.

> **Back-up prompts**
> These are some things the examiner may say to help you answer:
> *Talk about the people.*
> *Talk about the place.*
> *Talk about other things in the photograph.*

Part 3 (2–3 minutes)

In Part 3, the examiner asks you to do a task together. This is what the examiner says.

[*Turn to the task on page 200.*]

Now, in this part of the test, you're going to talk about something together for about two minutes. I'm going to describe a situation to you.

A man is moving to a new apartment in a different part of the city. The apartment is small but it has a balcony. His friends want to give him something useful for his new apartment.

Here are some things they could give him.

Talk together about the different things they could give the man, and say which would be best.

All right? Now, talk together.

 2–3 minutes

Thank you.

Part 4 (2–3 minutes)

In Part 4, the examiner asks you each a few questions about the topic in Part 3. For example, the examiner may ask you questions like:

- Do you like getting useful presents or fun presents? (Why?)
- Do you enjoy choosing presents for other people? (Why?/Why not?)
- Have you ever bought a present for a friend's new house or apartment? (Why?/Why not?)
- Have you lived in the same house or apartment for a long time? (Why?/Why not?)
- Do you think it's better to live in a city or in the countryside? (Why?)

> **Back-up prompts**
> The examiner may ask you
> to respond to your partner's
> answers, with questions like:
> *How/What about you?*
> *Do you agree?*
> *What do you think?*

 2–3 minutes

Thank you. That is the end of the test.

Part 1

Questions 1 – 5

For each question, choose the correct answer.

1

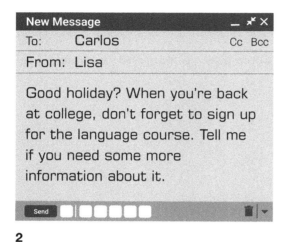

Why has Lisa contacted Carlos?

A   to tell him about her holiday

B   to remind him to do something

C   to give him some details

2

£30 TO RESERVE ANY PHOTOGRAPH IN THE EXHIBITION

A   You must pay £30 if you want to display photographs.

B   We will keep a photograph for you if you pay £30.

C   Some of the photos in the exhibition are reserved.

3

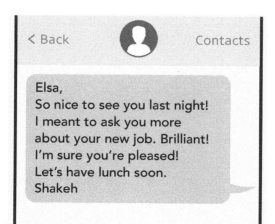

What is Shakeh doing in this text message?

A   offering Elsa her congratulations

B   providing some new information

C   thanking Elsa for her lunch

4

COLLEGE HOLIDAYS

After next Thursday, the Study Centre will be closed during evenings and weekends.

The Study Centre will

A   open again for students on Thursday.

B   open for fewer hours until Thursday.

C   change its opening hours from Thursday.

TIP STRIP

Question 4: The important word is 'after'. Which preposition matches this in the options? What will happen *after* Thursday?

Question 5: Does Keiko feel positive or negative about the hotel?

5

We're staying at the Regent Hotel. It's not the one we tried to book first, but it doesn't matter; this one's actually nearer the beach – where I'm spending all my time!
Keiko

What does Keiko feel about the Regent Hotel?

A   She wishes it was closer to the beach.

B   She prefers another hotel to it.

C   She thinks it has an advantage.

Part 2

Questions 6 – 10

For each question, choose the correct answer.

The people below all want to watch a TV programme.

On page 45, there are descriptions of eight TV programmes.

Decide which programme would be most suitable for the people below.

6

Sofia and Martina are interested in dance. They like both modern and traditional ballet, and enjoy learning about the dancers' experiences and ideas. They often go out in the evening.

7

Charlie and Emma are very keen on nature, particularly wildlife and the Antarctic. They enjoy experts discussing environmental issues, but they don't like phone-in programmes.

8

Mason and Noah both go cycling every weekend, entering short- and long-distance races. They want to be as fit as possible and also learn about the history of cycle racing.

9

Dipak and Anika enjoy live arts, especially theatre and classical music concerts. They live in the countryside and cannot go to the city very often.

10

Emilia and Artur are interested in exploration, especially people who go on trips for the first time or in unusual ways. They would like to plan a trip themselves one day.

TV programmes

A Stage Sensational

Three young actors play in this new evening series about a drama club. Keen to escape from the traditional approach of the school, they develop their own modern style – but can they manage to show it in public performances?

B One Man and His Bike

The longest journey: whether this is your first viewing or you are returning to keep up-to-date, you'll be entertained by Harry Lomas's self-recorded commentary. Harry describes his strange experiences as he rides around the world on his old red bike, following routes nobody's tried before. Tonight he meets a bear.

C Animal Access

If you're concerned about green issues, if you care about wild animals, here's the programme for you. Join our panel discussion by phoning in with your questions or suggestions for keeping our planet safe for animals, and you could even win the top prize: a trip to Antarctica.

D Moving Story

Follow the joys and heartaches of a junior dance school's attempts to reach the national final championships in different styles. Every afternoon you can see an update of their progress and you can phone in your vote on individual performances.

E The Road to Success

An enjoyable biography of one of the fastest cyclists of all time. Mixing old sections of film with current interviews – and even the chance to phone in with your own questions about technique and so on – this programme will inspire you to ride faster yourself.

F The Last Paradise

The white frozen landscape of the South Pole is said to be the last place humans haven't damaged beyond repair. Watch the fascinating filming of native animals and birds. You'll feel you're there yourself with some of the never-before-used camera techniques.

G Perfect Performances

Whether your tastes are traditional or more modern, you'll love this celebration of plays and operas, each one performed to the highest standards and broadcast to your living room. Additional material about history and background is available interactively.

H Routes and Riding

For children and parents alike, this programme is designed to get children riding bikes, exploring the countryside, getting fitter and healthier, and learning more about the natural world around them. Special routes are shown for first-time riders.

Part 3

For each question, choose the correct answer.

Design

We might think of design as a recent thing: we wear 'designer' clothes and sunglasses, drive fancy cars and watch TV programmes about designing our own super-modern houses. Yet, design has accompanied humans throughout their history. Think of the Egyptian pyramids, for example, the earliest of which was designed at least 4500 years ago. No one could disagree that the pyramids are one of the most amazing designs known to man. Then there are scientific instruments and furniture technology. Almost everything around us has been designed: the chair you're sitting on, the brush you clean your teeth with, the mobile phone that is always in your hand.

Today's top designers are well-known and admired for what they do, especially when it comes to the fashion and home interiors industries. They make a lot of money, too. Whether or not you think this is fair when others, such as doctors and charity workers, are out there saving lives and helping people, doesn't make a difference. After all, every job has its place in the world. And although it may not be essential to have that gorgeous new jacket or the latest mobile phone, it does make our lives a little bit nicer.

Not only do we want things to look good, we need them to do what they're meant to do, too. And without doubt, good design makes things easier for us. Machines make the manufacturing of goods quick and efficient, 'smart' motorways tell us about traffic up ahead so we can plan another route, and architects dream up the most incredible ways to make the best use of space in our homes. How on earth did people manage without today's 'modern conveniences'?

Somehow, they did. Take sailors of the past, for example. What an amazing experience to manage to sail the globe with only the most basic of equipment and 'discover' new lands and people! Similar journeys today take far less time and are far more predictable. Ships are filled with computers that help them to avoid the worst of the weather, and high-tech cruise ships look more like luxury hotels. Their passengers can relax, be entertained and watch the world go by in comfort.

11   The writer mentions the Egyptian pyramids in order to explain

A   how attractive they are compared to today's designs.

B   how important they are to modern designers.

C   how well they were designed for the period.

D   how long design has been around for.

12   What does the writer say about top designers?

A   They earn too much for what they do.

B   Their job is as important as other people's.

C   They aim to solve common problems people have.

D   Their work focuses on a limited number of products.

13   In the third paragraph, the writer says that

A   well-designed products work better than ones which aren't.

B   we expect products to have more than one purpose.

C   today's products can have complicated designs.

D   products of the past were not convenient to use.

14   What does the writer suggest in the final paragraph?

A   For some objects, appearance is less important than use.

B   Modern boats are designed to handle any weather condition.

C   Sea journeys were more exciting in the past.

D   Travellers on cruises have little knowledge of all the design around them.

15   A good conclusion for this article would be, 'Design has changed a lot since the days of the pyramids,

A   but the achievements of the past should not be forgotten.'

B   but designers still use some of the old design methods.'

C   but the basic ideas of style remain the same.'

D   but many of us do not pay attention to it.'

TIP STRIP

Question 11: Find where the Egyptian pyramids are first mentioned in the text. What does the writer say directly before this?

Question 12: The writer mentions all four options in some way but which one is his opinion?

Question 13: Read the whole of the third paragraph before choosing your answer. What does the writer actually say in the paragraph?

Question 14: 'Suggest' means that the writer does not clearly state his opinion. Read 'between the lines' to work out what he thinks.

Question 15: Think about what the whole text says before choosing your answer.

Questions 16 – 20

Five sentences have been removed from the text below.

For each question, choose the correct answer.

There are three extra sentences which you do not need to use.

TIP STRIP

Question 16: Look for
an option which answers
the previous questions.

Question 17: Find an
option which refers to
people: in this case, the
instructors.

Question 18: Which
option could be
connected to deciding
what to eat?

Question 19: What
could 'This includes'
after the gap refer to?

Question 20: Is there
an option which is
related to how many
people might take part
in a trip?

Blue Sky Cycling Tours

Wondering where to go away this summer? Want a holiday with excitement?

16 [ ] Join us on a Blue Sky Cycling Tour!

Our expert tour leaders will guide you along a carefully planned route and help you get fit while you relax. Not only are they great fun, but they are qualified fitness instructors, too. **17** [ ] The distance you cover each day will depend on the kind of countryside you're travelling through, and we'll make sure you never get too tired. Our routes include lots of places of interest, with frequent breaks to enjoy a coffee, a tour of an old castle or a swim in a lake!

What you eat is, of course, important when you're cycling for several hours a day! Each lunchtime you'll stop at a different village, where you'll be able to try local specialities. **18** [ ]

There's no need to worry about trying to carry your luggage on your bike, as our drivers will take this from hotel to hotel in our support cars, to be ready for you every night. Accommodation is arranged in good-quality hotels. **19** [ ] This includes single rooms for a small extra payment. Breakfast and dinner are provided, and there's a wide range of healthy meals to choose from.

In order to keep our tour groups friendly and safe, we limit the number of guests on each trip. **20** [ ] This means there is plenty of opportunity to get to know each other well, and make the most of your leaders' experience and knowledge. Young people over the age of fourteen are welcome on our trips, provided that they have a good level of fitness.

Contact us to make a booking!

A You definitely won't regret it!

B This means they'll make sure you cycle properly and prevent injury.

C We'll organise entry tickets for you in advance.

D Prices are per person, based on sharing, but other options are available.

E Our leaders will advise you on what you should have in order to keep your energy levels up.

F These are decisions that you must make by yourself.

G This may change depending on the difficulty of the route, but will reach no more than fifteen.

H If so, then the solution is right in front of you.

Part 5

Questions 21 – 26

For each question, choose the correct answer.

TIP STRIP

Question 21: The meaning you need is connected to what happens after something else has just happened.

Question 22: One of the verbs can be used to describe how a feeling is made.

Question 23: This is the only word which takes 'with' to form the meaning you need.

Question 24: Which word means 'understand' and can be used in this context?

Question 25: Which word forms part of the phrase 'the … of' to refer to time?

Question 26: Which word forms part of the phrase '… place' to mean 'happen'?

Music and feelings

It seems that music is almost as old as human life itself. If we knock two things together in time, like a stick and a drum, for example, we enjoy hearing the **(21)**................. . Music has meaning for humans and it has the power to change how we feel. It can make us excited – and it can **(22)**................. sad feelings. In our minds, we also **(23)**................. certain pieces of music with particular people or places. However, sometimes we almost do not **(24)**................. the effect that music has on us. For example, when you watch a TV programme or a film, there's often music playing – perhaps for the **(25)**................. of the time – and it tells you, though not directly, that something dangerous is about to **(26)**................. place, or that this is a romantic moment, and so on. But many people hardly remember the music when they've finished watching the programme.

21	A	result	B	end	C	final	D	answer
22	A	form	B	invent	C	discover	D	create
23	A	join	B	add	C	connect	D	fix
24	A	realise	B	know	C	follow	D	find
25	A	main	B	majority	C	most	D	maximum
26	A	make	B	have	C	take	D	get

Questions 27 – 32

For each question, write the correct answer.

Write **one** word for each gap.

The benefits of broccoli

By Flora Brown, Class 10B

Some people say they love the taste of broccoli, while others – like me – think it's bitter. But whatever we think of this vegetable, experts agree that it's healthy. **(27)**_____ fact, they say it's really good for us.

Experts are trying to decide whether or **(28)**_____ broccoli is a 'superfood' – a food which is especially good for our bodies. This hasn't been decided yet, but the list of benefits broccoli provides is pretty amazing. That's because, like lots of other green vegetables, it's full of good things. They say that as long **(29)**_____ we eat plenty of it, broccoli is probably able **(30)**_____ reduce heart disease, keep our bones strong and help our eyesight.

One question that **(31)**_____ often asked by people like me about vegetables like broccoli is, 'Are they better for us when they are cooked or raw?' Research shows that **(32)**_____ method of cooking broccoli is fine – it's the quantity that is important.

TIP STRIP

Question 27: The word you need forms part of a phrase with 'fact', meaning 'actually'.

Question 28: The word you need forms part of a phrase with 'whether or'.

Question 29: The word you need forms part of a phrase with 'as long', meaning 'if'.

Question 30: The word you need here completes the verb form 'be able …'

Question 31: Look at the verb form after the gap. What kind of tense is this?

Question 32: The word you need means that both raw and cooked broccoli is OK.

Part 1

You **must** answer this question.

Write your answer in about **100 words**.

Question 1

Read this email from your English-speaking friend Alex and the notes you have made.

From:	Alex
Subject:	My sister's birthday

Hi

It's my sister Anna's birthday next week! I'm excited about celebrating ◄········ *Me too!*
with her on Saturday.

You said you wouldn't mind helping me choose a present for her. Are ◄········ *Yes – suggest where to go shopping*
you free tomorrow morning to come shopping with me?

I have a couple of ideas for presents. Do you think it's a good idea to
buy her something to wear, or should I just get her a £20 gift card so ◄········ *Explain*
she can spend it on what she wants?

Shall we have lunch together after shopping? ◄········ *Sorry, but …*

Anyway, let me know!

Alex

Write your **email** to Alex using **all the notes**.

Part 2

Choose **one** of these questions.

Write your answer in about **100 words**.

Question 2

You see this announcement on an English-language website.

> ### Articles wanted!
> #### *A great computer game*
> What computer game do you most enjoy playing? What do you like about it? Do you think it is better to play computer games alone or with other competitors? Why?
>
> Write an article answering these questions. We will publish the best articles on our website!

Write your **article**.

Question 3

Your English teacher has asked you to write a story.
Your story must begin with this sentence.

The clouds over the sea were getting darker.

Write your **story**.

TIP STRIP

Question 1:

- Remember that you are writing to a friend. Should your email be formal or informal?
- Start and end your email in an appropriate way and use full sentences.
- Plan your answer: which piece of information will you put in each paragraph?
- Remember to write about all the points in the notes!

Question 2:

- Answer all of the questions in the task.
- Connect your ideas together to create an interesting article. Remember to use paragraphs.
- Think about what you'd like to say and don't repeat information.

Question 3:

- Plan your story: What happened next? How does the story end?
- Use a range of language. It will make your story more interesting for the reader.

Part I

Questions 1 – 7

For each question, choose the correct answer.

---

1 Which is the family's holiday house?

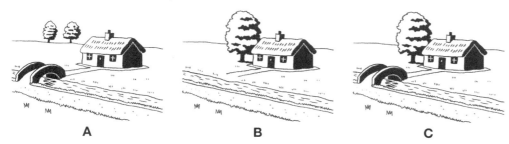

A   B   C

2 What sport has just become available at the sports centre?

A   B   C

3 Where is the man's wallet?

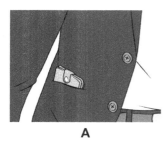 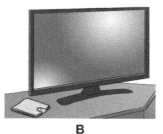 

A   B   C

TIP STRIP

Question 1: Look at the different items in the pictures: the house, the trees, the river, the bridge. What do people do there?

Question 2: Listen for what has just become available, not what is already available or coming in the future.

Question 3: You may need to remember the first part of what the man says, so listen carefully.

4 When did David's aunt leave?

A B C

5 Which photo are they talking about?

A B C

6 What will the woman take on the train journey?

A B C

7 How much will the boy pay for a ticket for the football match?

A B C

Questions 8 – 13

For each question, choose the correct answer.

---

8   You will hear two friends talking about free-time activities.
What does the man like doing?

   A   individual activities

   B   sociable activities

   C   exercise activities

9   You will hear two friends talking about biking.
How do they both feel about their next bike ride?

   A   nervous about where it will take place

   B   worried that it will be too long

   C   anxious about trying new bikes

10   You will hear two friends talking about growing up in the countryside.
What did the woman like about it?

   A   seeing the attractive landscape

   B   learning about animals

   C   spending time outside

11   You will hear two friends talking about a concert they have been to.
What do they agree about?

   A   how good the concert hall was

   B   how good the singer was

   C   how good the sound was

12   You will hear two friends talking about some university work.
Why is the man talking to his friend?

   A   to remind her to check something

   B   to warn her to arrange something correctly

   C   to ask her to lend him something

13   You will hear two colleagues talking about their work.
How does the woman feel about her new job?

   A   amazed by how friendly people are

   B   curious about the work she will have to do

   C   grateful for the help she has received

TIP STRIP

Question 8: The man refers to all three kinds of activities, but he only does one of them.

Question 9: Listen for what they both feel.

Question 10: The woman didn't enjoy two of the three options. Listen for a phrase which introduces what she did like.

Question 11: The woman uses words and phrases to express agreement. Listen for the word/phrase which is used to agree with one of the man's opinions.

Question 12: You won't hear the verbs in the options, so listen carefully to what the man is doing.

Question 13: The woman doesn't use any of the adjectives in the options, so you have to work out how she feels from what she says.

Part 3

Questions 14 – 19

For each question, write the correct answer in the gap. Write **one** or **two words** or a **number** or a **date** or a **time**

You will hear a man giving a talk about a sports event to raise money for charity.

Mini Olympic Games

Location: Greenford Primary School

Closing date for entries: **(14)**..................

Aims: – to raise money for research and a new **(15)**..................

      – to encourage children in sport

First event starts: **(16)**..................

Parents: make sure children have enough **(17)**.................. on the day

Most popular event expected to be the **(18)**..................

More children needed for the **(19)**.................. event

TIP STRIP

Question 14: You will hear more than one date. The date you need is the last date you can apply to take part.

Question 15: The words in the recording are not the same as the words in the question, but they have the same meaning.

Question 16: Listen for a time. You will hear three times, but you need to choose the correct one.

Question 17: One thing is provided, but parents have to bring something themselves.

Question 18: You will hear different events. Listen for another way to say 'most popular'.

Question 19: Listen for the event that doesn't have enough people yet.

Part 4

Questions 20 – 25

For each question, choose the correct answer.

_____

You will hear a radio interview with a woman called Tina about her recent trip to Africa.

20 What does Tina say about the weather during her trip?

    A   It rained almost every day.

    B   It was too hot during the day.

    C   It was very cold at night.

21 The first journey Tina made was

    A   in a small plane.

    B   on foot.

    C   by a special car.

22 On the second day, Tina felt

    A   nervous about seeing a lion.

    B   excited to see a giraffe.

    C   surprised to see a monkey.

23 Tina liked how close she got to

    A   a group of elephants.

    B   some wild dogs.

    C   different birds.

24 Who does Tina think would most enjoy a trip to Zambia?

    A   young people on a break from university

    B   couples with young children

    C   retired people who have more time to travel

25 Tina says she will never forget

    A   the beautiful sunsets she saw each day.

    B   the interesting people she met.

    C   the sense of space she experienced.

TIP STRIP

Question 20: Listen for the time of year when Tina went to Africa.

Question 21: The important word to listen out for here means 'first'.

Question 22: Listen to how Tina felt when she went to look for animals on the second day.

Question 23: Are there other ways to say 'close to'?

Question 24: 'Most' is the important idea in this question.

Question 25: Listen out for a phrase which means the same as 'never forget'.

Part 1 (2–3 minutes)

Phase 1

- What's your name?
- Where do you live?

- Do you work or are you a student?
- What do you do/study?

TIP STRIP

Part 1 Phase 1

Talk to the examiner in this part, not your partner.

Always answer in full sentences.

Add a little extra information to your answers, but don't say too much. Give shorter answers in this part.
You can practise your answers before the test, but don't memorise them. Your answers must sound natural.

Phase 2

- What did you do yesterday evening?
- Tell me about the people you live with.

- What places would you like to visit in the future?
- What kind of music do you like listening to?

TIP STRIP

Part 1 Phase 2

Talk to the examiner in this part, not your partner.

Give longer answers. Try to add extra information like reasons, examples and other interesting details.

The questions are always about you. Be prepared to talk about things like your hobbies and interests, your likes and dislikes, your studies, and so on.

TIP STRIP

Part 2

Start with a simple, general description of the situation: say where the people are and what is happening.

Then describe the photo in more detail. Talk about what the people are doing, what they are wearing, how you think they are feeling, where the different objects are, etc.

Imagine the examiner can't see the photo – describe it in as much detail as you can.

If you don't know a word, try to describe it (e.g. *It's something you use for …*).

Give reasons for your ideas and opinions (e.g. *I think they're happy because …*).

Try to keep talking until the examiner stops you.

Part 2 (2–3 minutes)

2A Playing a video game

Now, I'd like each of you to talk on your own about something.
I'm going to give each of you a photograph and I'd like you to talk about it.

A, here is your photograph. It shows **people playing a video game**.
[*Turn to photograph 2A on page 192.*]
B, you just listen.
A, please tell us what you can see in the photograph.

🕑 about 1 minute

Thank you.

2B Learning

B, here is your photograph. It shows **people learning something**.
[*Turn to photograph 2B on page 196.*]
A, you just listen.
B, please tell us what you can see in the photograph.

🕑 about 1 minute

Thank you.

Part 3 (2–3 minutes)

Now, in this part of the test, you're going to talk about something together for about two minutes. I'm going to describe a situation to you.

[*Turn to the task on page 201.*]

A school has got some money to buy more equipment to help its students.

Here are some things the school could buy.

Talk together about the different things the school could buy and say which would be most useful for the students.

All right? Now, talk together.

 2–3 minutes

Thank you.

Part 4 (2–3 minutes)

- Do/Did you enjoy doing sport at school? (Why?/Why not?)
- How do/did you travel to school? (Why?)
- Do you prefer learning new things alone or with other people? (Why?)
- Is it useful to learn new skills in your free time? (Why?/Why not?)
- Do you think people spend too much time working and studying these days? (Why?/Why not?)

 2–3 minutes

Thank you. That is the end of the test.

Part 1

Questions 1 – 5

For each question, choose the correct answer.

1

SPORTS CLUB GYM

Please put all practice equipment back in this room before you leave.

A   Remember to take your equipment with you when you leave.

B   You shouldn't take any equipment outside this room when you go.

C   We leave some equipment at the back of this room for practising.

2

< Back   Contacts

I'm here in London today with Chris, who's at a job interview at the moment. It's raining, so I'm visiting museums. We're catching the train home together tonight. Jenny

A   Chris is staying overnight in London, but Jenny isn't.

B   Jenny is writing this text while Chris attends an interview.

C   Jenny and Chris are spending the day together sightseeing.

3

GREAT SPORTS BIKE

In perfect condition, less than two years old

Quick sale needed – offers welcome (not less than €100)

Abdul 0775 221 321

A   Abdul's bike needs only a few repairs.

B   Abdul bought this bike two years ago.

C   Abdul would accept €100 for his bike.

4

Shop delivery vehicles
unload here
08.00 a.m. – 10.00 a.m. daily
Customer parking permitted
at any other time

A Customers may park here when vehicles are not unloading.

B Customers may park outside the shop for up to two hours.

C You may unload your delivery vehicle here after ten o'clock.

5

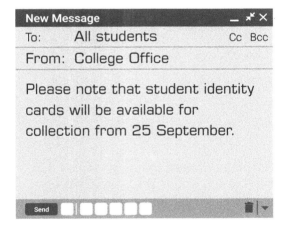

New Message

To: All students   Cc Bcc

From: College Office

Please note that student identity cards will be available for collection from 25 September.

Send

A Students should bring their identity cards with them on 25 September.

B Student identity cards are only available until 25 September.

C The first day students can pick up identity cards is 25 September.

Part 2

Questions 6 – 10

For each question, choose the correct answer.

The people below all want to do a training course.

On page 63 there are eight advertisements for training courses.

Decide which training course would be the most suitable for the people below.

6  Heinrich studies economics at university but has decided he wants to work in the media in future. His economics lectures are in the mornings and he goes to nightclubs most evenings.

7  Anika works in a fashionable clothes shop and would like to become a manager there, but she needs to improve her ability to use computers. The shop is open every day until 6 p.m.

8  Abigail doesn't have a job at the moment, but she would like to work in a sports centre, perhaps as a coach to a team. She is keen on keeping fit and swims every day.

9  Lin wants to learn more about business so that he can run his own shop one day. He's studying languages at university and has a part-time job as an assistant in a sports shop.

10  Lena is interested in style and fashion, particularly interior design. Her current job is in a music shop, where she works every evening.

Training courses

A On this useful course, you'll learn how to manage others and bring out the best in any group. The course is relevant to a wide range of work situations, particularly hospitality, sports and entertainment. It's a full-time and demanding course, with expert teachers and proven results.

B High street or street market, clothes, furniture or jewellery: whatever you sell, you can learn to sell more of it. The internet is still largely misunderstood by most business people, so make sure you're ahead of the game with this evening course in IT systems and online selling, and improve your chances of success.

C Music is a fashionable business to be in right now, and you can increase your chances by learning some important techniques. With our special course structure, you can choose when and where to study, putting you firmly on the path to success.

D Use our computer-based course to help you achieve your dreams. Fashion is an international language, but you need language skills to succeed in it. Our specialist course will provide you with valuable practice, so you can communicate your creative ideas.

E Sport and leisure are growing parts of the economy at present. You can ensure your place in their future with our special international sports sector certificate course, which includes important topics such as marketing, and health and safety for sports centre management. You need to have relevant employment experience.

F Are you creative? Are you ambitious? This course will help you get ahead in the competitive world of creative business, where you need to be super-fit to win. Join our course of morning classes and learn how to start up a business – perhaps a shop or consultancy.

G This course is perfect for people who have a basic understanding of business but who want to explore the possibilities of TV, newspapers, the internet and so on as their career. This is a part-time course, with classes three afternoons a week.

H Do you wish to be your own boss? Need to know how? Many ambitious and skilled people find they have some experience and perhaps a strong academic background, but feel they need specific knowledge about marketing and finance to ensure their success when selling to the public.

Questions 11 – 15

For each question, choose the correct answer.

My job: John Knight, architect

I'm an architect and I love my job. At school, I didn't have much idea what I might do afterwards. I enjoyed science and art, and got on well with my teachers, who often lent me extra books on topics I was interested in. But when I was about to leave school and still didn't know what I wanted to study at university, my mum and dad said they thought I should consider training as an architect. I realised then that designing buildings might indeed be the perfect job for me.

And it is. It's a great job, connecting engineering, art, people and the places we all live and work in. Clients – our word for customers – are the ones who make it all happen. Some I get on with, some not. I have to balance what they say they'd like the final result to be – and they're usually very certain about that – with what is or isn't actually possible. I invite them to explain the project as they see it developing and then try to explore ways forward from there.

I love most things about my job. There are a lot of meetings to attend, of course, all over the country. Then there's the designing itself, and also the research, the checking, dealing with builders and so on. And I'm developing all the time as a professional, learning new ways of doing things. Above all, it's the good mix of activities. I also attend conferences to give lectures about my work, which is a great opportunity to meet other architects. Their experiences and ideas teach me so much.

Ever since I started out as a young architect, I've tried not to look back, but to keep finding new solutions. I've designed all sorts of buildings, with my favourite so far being a hospital – which is basically a hotel for the ill – and I think I'm very likely to get the contract for a new intercity station that will be built on the site of an old museum in the centre of the city where I live.

11   What gave John the idea of becoming an architect?

    A   His art teacher suggested he should do it.

    B   His parents recommended it as an option.

    C   He was good at science subjects at school.

    D   He enjoyed looking at books about buildings.

12   John says that people who employ him as an architect often

    A   end up being difficult to work with.

    B   change their minds about their plans.

    C   have clear ideas about what they expect.

    D   have realistic ideas about what is possible.

13   What does John like most about his work?

    A   He can travel to different places.

    B   He is always learning new things.

    C   He meets a lot of different people.

    D   He does a variety of different things.

14   In the fourth paragraph, John says he feels

    A   excited about a hospital he's going to build.

    B   hopeful that he'll be able to design a station.

    C   disappointed that a museum has been closed.

    D   pleased that his ideas for a hotel were popular.

15   What would one of John's colleagues say about him?

    A

> He sometimes feels annoyed with the people he designs for, but he always communicates with them and listens to them while working on their project.

    B

> He likes to compare different buildings he's designed with each other, to see if this gives him new ideas.

    C

> He'd intended to do a different job, but he's learnt to enjoy his work and has got better at working in a team.

    D

> He believes he produced his most interesting designs when he was young and keen to do more challenging jobs.

Part 4

Questions 16 – 20

Five sentences have been removed from the text below.

For each question, choose the correct answer.

There are three extra sentences which you do not need to use.

Taking selfies

Many people love taking photographs, and loads of the pictures people take these days are selfies – pictures of themselves. You may imagine that selfies are something new and didn't exist before the invention of smartphones. **16** [   ]

The earliest known self-portrait photograph – possibly the world's first selfie – was taken in 1839 in the United States by a man called Robert Cornelius. He didn't do it so he could send pictures of himself to friends and family. **17** [   ] He wanted to show that the recently invented 'daguerreotype process' could be used to take portrait photographs. In order to get the picture, Cornelius had to set up the camera then run to a seat in front of it and remain completely still for possibly as long as fifteen minutes. Selfies might not be so popular if people still had to do that every time!

18 [   ] For instance, in 1954 Jackie Kennedy took a photo in the mirror – a 'mirror selfie' – of herself, her husband – the future US president John F. Kennedy – and his sister Ethel. And US astronaut Buzz Aldrin took a picture of himself in 1966.

19 [   ] At the time he took the selfie, he was walking on the Moon.

Mirror selfies like the Kennedy photograph have been popular since cameras became more widely available to the public in the early 1900s. Many of these pictures can still be seen in photo libraries and museums today, as well as online.

20 [   ] However, being able to see which cameras they used to take their pictures provides useful information for anyone studying the history of photography. And no doubt the pictures we take today will interest people in 100 years' time, for a variety of reasons.

A   After all that effort, he finally managed to take a good picture.

B   There are many more examples of famous early selfies.

C   That was how they achieved such an interesting effect.

D   In fact, they are a lot older than many people think.

E   The identity of the people in them is often a mystery.

F   What made this one particularly special was the location.

G   They are really interesting because they show us their daily lives.

H   His aim was actually to test a new photographic method.

Part 5

Questions 21 – 26

For each question, choose the correct answer.

Sharks

There are more than 1000 species of shark and new ones are discovered every year. Some sharks swim great **(21)** .... to find food, others don't. Some live alone and others live in groups. It can take some sharks up to fifteen years to **(22)** .... adults.

The 1975 film *Jaws* **(23)** .... millions of people a fear of sharks. It was about a Great White Shark, the largest of all sharks. Some of them are over 3 m long and they can weigh up to 3000 kg.

People shouldn't be so scared of sharks, however. Humans aren't **(24)** .... to sharks as food because sharks prefer animals with more fat and less bone. When sharks attack humans, it's usually because they **(25)** .... they are another kind of animal, like a seal, for example. In fact, it's humans who are a danger to sharks, killing them in huge **(26)** .... every year.

21	A	lengths	B	distances	C	routes	D	journeys
22	A	reach	B	arrive	C	grow	D	become
23	A	gave	B	made	C	left	D	put
24	A	beautiful	B	attractive	C	delighted	D	favourite
25	A	know	B	notice	C	think	D	realise
26	A	numbers	B	totals	C	sums	D	averages

Questions 27 – 32

For each question, write the correct answer.

Write **one** word for each gap.

Town museum

The museum in my town has just opened again after six months. It looks the same from outside, but inside it's very different! There are now six large rooms instead **(27)** .... the twelve smaller rooms that there **(28)** .... to be, so it feels much lighter and brighter. Although most of the objects are **(29)** .... same, the labels describing them are all new.

I went **(30)** .... weekend, and I loved the way the displays **(31)** .... organised. It was much easier to see everything and understand what I was looking at. There's also a wonderful exhibition of old paintings of our town.

I also liked the new café, with its colourful furniture and delicious food. The cake I had was **(32)** .... good that I just had to have a second piece! Next time you have a free hour or two, go and see for yourself. I'm sure you'll love it too!

Part 1

You **must** answer this question.

Write your answer in about **100 words**.

Question 1

Read this email from your English-speaking friend Dani and the notes you have made.

From: Dani

Subject: Picnic next week

Hi!

I'm really looking forward to our picnic next week! We could have the picnic in the park or maybe have it somewhere else. Where would you prefer?

My brother and his wife and their four young children have asked me if they can join us. Do you think that's a good idea?

After the picnic, we could go to the cinema if you like. Are you free to do that?

Write soon and let me know!

Dani

Me too!

Explain

Tell Dani

No, because ...

Write your **email** to Dani using **all the notes**.

Part 2

Choose **one** of these questions.

Write your answer in about **100 words**.

Question 2

You see this announcement in an English-language magazine.

> **Travel**
>
> How do you usually travel each day? Why do you use this kind of transport?
>
> Do you think that people should change the way they travel in your country in order to help the environment?
>
> The best article will win a prize!

Write your **article**.

Question 3

Your English teacher has asked you to write a story.

Your story must begin with this sentence.

I was walking through the shopping centre when someone called out my name.

Write your **story**.

Part I

Questions 1 – 7

For each question, choose the correct answer.

---

1 What did Juan enjoy on holiday?

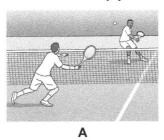
A

B

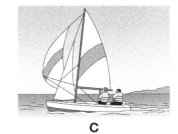
C

2 Where will the woman go first after work?

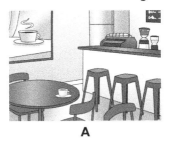
A

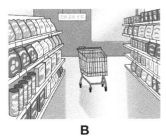
B

C

3 Which is the new flat?

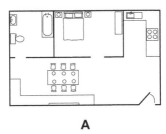
A

B

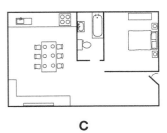
C

4   When do they decide to have lunch?

  A   B   C

5   Which jacket does Harry want to buy?

  A   B   C

6   Which postcard do they decide to send?

   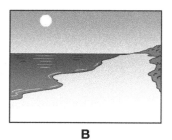   

  A   B   C

7   How will they travel to the airport?

      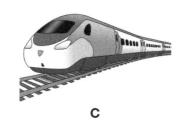

  A   B   C

Questions 8 – 13

For each question, choose the correct answer.

___

8   You will hear a man talking to a shop assistant about a laptop he wants to buy.
Why does he want this one?

   A   It's very light.

   B   It isn't very expensive.

   C   It has a long battery life.

9   You will hear two colleagues talking about a project they're working on.
What do they both hope?

   A   It will soon be finished.

   B   It will make them famous.

   C   It will help them get promoted.

10   You will hear a woman telling a friend about a restaurant.
What did she like about it?

   A   The food was delicious.

   B   The staff were efficient.

   C   The atmosphere was lively.

11   You will hear two friends talking about a football match.
What did the woman think about it?

   A   It was boring.

   B   The best team won.

   C   Some players weren't as good as usual.

12   You will hear a man telling a friend about his sister.
How does he describe her?

   A   She's creative.

   B   She's helpful.

   C   She's hard-working.

13   You will hear two students talking about a party they both went to.
Why were they disappointed?

   A   The music wasn't good.

   B   Not many of their friends were there.

   C   The place where it was held was too small.

Part 3

Questions 14 – 19

For each question, write the correct answer in the gap. Write **one** or **two words** or a **number** or a **date** or a **time**

You will hear a woman talking about a festival.

Honeyford Festival

Festival for town of Honeyford and surrounding countryside,

Honeyford Festival was first held in the year **(14)** ....

Last year there were record numbers of **(15)** ....

A TV programme crew will film the show of traditional **(16)** ....

There will be a demonstration of making **(17)** ....

You can take part in a **(18)** .... class.

A family ticket costs **(19)** £................... .

Part 4

For each question, choose the correct answer.

_____

You will hear an interview with a man called Robbie, who works as a courier delivering things by bicycle in London.

20   Robbie became a bike courier because

    A   he didn't like being a student.

    B   his friends encouraged him.

    C   he was unable to find another job.

21   What happened when he went for his interview?

    A   He arrived very late.

    B   It was difficult to find the office.

    C   Everybody seemed very friendly.

22   What was a problem on his first day?

    A   A parcel was too big to carry.

    B   His bike broke down.

    C   He went to the wrong address.

23   Robbie thinks that many riders feel

    A   competitive.

    B   independent.

    C   stressed.

24   Robbie says many couriers are surprised that they don't

    A   learn more about the geography of London.

    B   spend much time with the other couriers.

    C   get as tired as they had expected to.

25   What advice does Robbie give about becoming a bicycle courier?

    A   Make sure you have a very good bike.

    B   Do it for a limited period of time.

    C   Study a street map of London.

Part 1 (2–3 minutes)

Phase 1

- What's your name?
- Where do you live?
- Do you work or are you a student?
- What do you do/study?

Phase 2

- What do you enjoy about learning English?
- Tell me about what you do in your free time.
- How often do you use a mobile phone?
- Which part of the day do you like best, the morning or the evening?

Part 2 (2–3 minutes)

3A Studying

Now, I'd like each of you to talk on your own about something.
I'm going to give each of you a photograph, and I'd like you to talk about it.

A, here is your photograph. It shows **people studying**.
[*Turn to photograph 3A on page 193.*]
B, you just listen.
A, please tell us what you can see in the photograph.

🕑 about 1 minute

Thank you.

3B Practising

B, here is your photograph. It shows **people practising**.
[*Turn to photograph 3B on page 197.*]
A, you just listen.
B, please tell us what you can see in the photograph.

🕑 about 1 minute

Thank you.

Part 3 (2–3 minutes)

Now, in this part of the test, you're going to talk about something together for about two minutes. I'm going to describe a situation to you.

[*Turn to the task on page 202.*]

A young woman is going to the UK to study for six months. Her friends want to give her a present.

Here are some things they could give her.

Talk together about the different presents and say which would be the most useful.

All right? Now, talk together.

 2–3 minutes

Thank you.

Part 4 (2–3 minutes)

- What do you usually take with you when you travel somewhere? Why?
- Which country would you most like to visit? Why?
- What do you like doing when you visit new places? Why?
- Is it better to visit a big city or the seaside? Why?
- How important is it to speak the language of a country you are visiting? Why?

 2–3 minutes

Thank you. That is the end of the test.

TEST 4

Part 1

Questions 1 – 5

For each question, choose the correct answer.

1

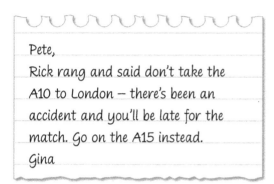

Pete,
Rick rang and said don't take the A10 to London – there's been an accident and you'll be late for the match. Go on the A15 instead.
Gina

A Pete needs to change route to arrive earlier.

B Gina will come to the match if there's enough time.

C Pete should take the A10 to save time.

2

New Message

To: Andre   Cc Bcc
From: Ali

Martina's coming next weekend, so we're hiring a river boat. Do you want to join us? We need you to translate and you could help cook!

Send

What does Ali want Andre to do?

A Make all the meals on holiday.

B Help everybody communicate.

C Find a good river boat to hire.

3

GOODLIFE FITNESS CLUB

Special offer for existing members:

Introduce a friend to the club and receive free sports clothes!

Your friend must pay a twelve-month fee.

A You must pay your twelve-month membership fee for Goodlife now.

B Goodlife is selling sports clothes to members at special prices.

C You can get a gift if you persuade a friend to join Goodlife.

4

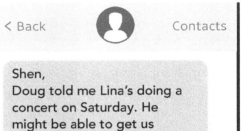

< Back   Contacts

Shen,
Doug told me Lina's doing a concert on Saturday. He might be able to get us tickets, so let him know if you want to see her play.
Kim

Who should Shen contact if she wants to see the concert?

A   Kim

B   Lina

C   Doug

5

To be taken between meals at four-hourly intervals, up to four times daily.

If taking this medicine, you must

A   eat just before you take it.

B   wait four hours before taking it again.

C   take it at least four times a day.

Part 2

Questions 6 – 10

For each question, choose the correct answer.

___

The people below all want to visit a music website.

On page 81, there are reviews of eight music websites.

Decide which website would be most suitable for the people below.

6  Ravi is interested in a wide range of musical styles. He doesn't have much money to spend on buying music for himself, but he likes buying it as a present for friends and family.

7  Leila is very keen on dance music from the 1950s and 1960s, although she knows this kind of music is hard to find and expensive to buy.

8  Takumi enjoys going to concerts of various types of music, although he finds that tickets are very expensive. He likes buying music gift cards as presents to friends.

9  Ijeoma likes to listen to music while she's studying. She would like to work in the music industry in the future. She buys music as often as she can afford it.

10  Liam studies music at university. He goes to traditional and modern dance performances when he can afford to. He listens to music when he is running in the park.

Music sites on the web

A   This is a very useful website and I certainly recommend it to music lovers with a taste for the tunes and songs of the dance halls in the middle of the last century. If you're looking for something that's not available elsewhere or if you'd like to listen to parts of those old favourites for free, try here.

B   This music website caters to all tastes. From early jazz through 1970s pop to current world music, you should be able to buy what you want here. Many songs are available to listen to for free, and there's some reasonably priced music, with an efficient present-ordering service.

C   If you're hungry for live music, this is probably the best site for you. There's a comprehensive guide to all concerts every night, from the large classical shows to the small upstairs blues rooms. What's more, there are plenty of discounts, from half-price entrance to shows, to 10 percent off online music purchases.

D   This site says it's by musicians for musicians, with a focus on current dance music. There are lots of requests for new musicians to join new bands, and there are advertisements for performances, but the information is sometimes a little out of date. Worth a look though.

E   This interesting site is packed with information about all kinds of music, including articles about finding a job in the music business. As well as selling a good range of music at fair prices, they also offer a free playlist, so you can put together hours of free listening to download.

F   This is mainly a review site, so want-to-be journalists can send in their reviews of concerts, albums and so on. The standard is pretty high, as most people who send in reviews are music students or musicians themselves.

G   This is an unusual site and will be just right for you if dance is what you like. You can save money with cheap tickets to see old and new ballet. There are playlists you stream on your phone and articles about ballet's history, although these are a bit serious.

H   This site claims it can find you any ticket for any dance performance, although this service doesn't come cheap. They also claim they can find any record or CD ever recorded, though this claim may be harder to prove. Either way, they're great, but far from cheap.

Part 3

Questions 11 – 15

For each question, choose the correct answer.

Learning about learning languages

by Davide Montrois

In many ways, my interest in language learning began with my grandmother. She had moved from Switzerland to England when she was a young adult and I was always amazed by the way she spoke English to me, Italian to my grandfather and Swiss French or German on the phone to relatives and friends back home. She was truly multilingual. I always imagined she could be a translator of books, or even a tour guide, as she seemed to have such skill with languages. Amazingly, she hadn't learnt English at school, but had picked it up by herself when she came to England.

The main reason my grandmother continued to speak so many languages was so she could communicate with all the people she knew in different cultures. Although I can speak a bit of Italian and German from listening to her, I only know basic grammar and sometimes get confused between words, so it's hard for me to understand how someone can speak several languages so well. I'd love to know how my grandmother does it!

Although it's often said that learning languages can help you to find higher-paid employment, English has developed as a global language, used for international communication by people in all kinds of social groups. I rarely use anything else in my own job, and though I don't need another language, being able to ask for a meal in a restaurant on holiday would be useful. More than anything, it would be nice to chat with people across the world – it's easy to make new friends online that way.

In fact, language learning is easier now than ever. There's extra help from new technology, for example. Recording your voice with feedback facilities on web learning sites helps you to see how well you're doing and continue to improve. There are apps to help you learn new words, and audio technology is used in language classes. I still think going to class improves conversation skills and helps you deal quickly with mistakes. It's good to combine methods.

Or you can just spend a little time talking to my grandmother!

11 The purpose of the first paragraph is to introduce the writer's grandmother's

    A   unusual way of life.

    B   language background.

    C   varied career.

    D   interesting family.

12 How does the writer feel about his grandmother's language skills?

    A   hopeful of one day being as good as she is

    B   amazed by how quickly she can learn languages

    C   curious about how she is able to speak so many languages

    D   proud of how easily she can have conversations with other people

13 The writer would like to know more languages in order to

    A   learn more about cultures he finds interesting.

    B   do more international travel.

    C   get a better job.

    D   communicate with people in other countries.

14 The writer says new technology helps people learn languages because they can

    A   check their progress.

    B   study in different places.

    C   chat to other learners.

    D   avoid repeating mistakes.

15 What would the writer say to one of his friends?

    A

> It was my grandmother who helped me learn so many different languages. She's amazing!

    B

> I'm thinking of signing up for a language course to help me learn useful phrases before I go to Spain.

    C

> I've always found it easy learning languages. Words just seem to stay in my head somehow.

    D

> I am just finishing a professional translation project and my grandmother is checking it for me.

Part 4

Questions 16 – 20

Five sentences have been removed from the text below.

For each question, choose the correct answer.

There are three extra sentences which you do not need to use.

Heltonbrook Town Council

'What's on' webpage

This is the place to find out what's happening around town this month. This site was started just a few weeks ago, in response to requests from people living in the area who were worried about the environmental costs of the town council's printed magazine. **16** [ ]

Heltonbrook is a popular town, with plenty to offer both the people who live here and the many visitors we receive every year. **17** [ ] This includes reviews of, and information about, restaurants, hotels, and leisure and entertainment venues.

Sports Day

14 July will see Heltonbrook's first Sports Day, organised by the council and something we hope will become a regular event in the town's calendar. There will be all kinds of sporting events. Judges will include Greg Davids, our local sailing champion, and Tim Progue, Head Teacher at Northfields School. **18** [ ] These include a 1500-metre running race, horse-riding and high diving. The list is a long one! For details on how to enter, contact us via the 'Contact us' page. Please note the closing date is 11 July.

Arts Show

The Heltonbrook Arts Show is already well-known in our region, where it is the biggest temporary collection of art, with over 3000 paintings by local artists. **19** [ ] This means you can take something home with you on the day itself! There will be a vote, open to all who attend the show, to decide the single best picture. The show is open daily from 15–18 July.

Open Spaces

Don't forget this year's 'Open Spaces'. This special feature of Heltonbrook life will run during the last week of July. **20** [ ] Beautiful gardens, ancient buildings and the old college library are just a few examples. Each year more places are added to the list.

A   But don't forget – time is already running out!

B   As a responsible organisation, we set up this webpage instead, to solve
this problem.

C   But what's really special about it is that everything on display is available at very
reasonable prices.

D   See the 'When and Where' page for details about meeting times and places.

E   Together, they will hand out prizes to the winners of events.

F   All sorts of hidden places will give residents and visitors the chance to see what
they normally can't.

G   We hope you will be able to bring something of your own along.

H   With the numbers of these increasing, we, the council, aim to provide everything
they need.

Part 5

Questions 21 – 26

For each question, choose the correct answer.

Rice

Rice has been an important food in Asia and Africa for over 3000 years. Farmers can **(21)** .... several crops of rice in a single year, and it is quite cheap to grow. It is also possible to **(22)** .... uncooked rice for a long time, so it can be a useful food for people who don't have fridges.

Rice is grown and eaten in many different countries and it is a basic **(23)** .... of the diet of billions of people on Earth. Some may have rice with vegetables for their meal, while others may eat it with fish or meat. Rice is often **(24)** .... in water, but every culture has its own special **(25)** .... of cooking it. Some people stir rice while it is in the pan, for example, while others say you mustn't **(26)** .... it when it is cooking.

21	**A**	produce	**B**	design	**C**	make	**D**	create
22	**A**	continue	**B**	stay	**C**	keep	**D**	hold
23	**A**	place	**B**	piece	**C**	point	**D**	part
24	**A**	grilled	**B**	boiled	**C**	roasted	**D**	fried
25	**A**	way	**B**	pattern	**C**	route	**D**	plan
26	**A**	deal	**B**	contact	**C**	touch	**D**	manage

Part 6

Questions 27 – 32

For each question, write the correct answer.

Write **one** word for each gap.

Collecting things

I've collected all kinds of things over the years: stones I found on the beach, books, even experiences! I started thinking about **(27)** .... makes people want to collect and here are my ideas.

For me, collecting reminds me **(28)** .... my childhood. That might be true for other people, who collect interesting toys or continue with a collection they started when they **(29)** .... young. A friend of mine enjoys the feeling of finding a rare or valuable item which other collectors he knows don't have. Collecting can also be a good way to relax and help us forget about everyday problems, just **(30)** .... other hobbies can.

I know a few people who collect different things **(31)** .... as teddy bears, which my best friend collects, and I know someone else **(32)** .... likes clocks. Even the local museum has collections of ancient coins. It seems that collecting is a really popular thing to do!

Part 1

You **must** answer this question.

Write your answer in about **100 words**.

Question 1

Read this email from your English-speaking friend Lin and the notes you have made.

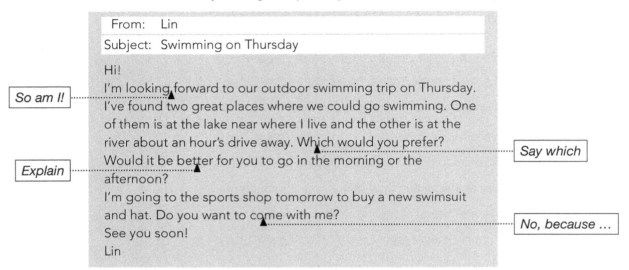

So am I!

Explain

From: Lin

Subject: Swimming on Thursday

Hi!
I'm looking forward to our outdoor swimming trip on Thursday.
I've found two great places where we could go swimming. One
of them is at the lake near where I live and the other is at the
river about an hour's drive away. Which would you prefer?
Would it be better for you to go in the morning or the
afternoon?
I'm going to the sports shop tomorrow to buy a new swimsuit
and hat. Do you want to come with me?
See you soon!
Lin

Say which

No, because ...

Write your **email** to Lin using **all the notes**.

Part 2

Choose **one** of these questions.

Write your answer in about **100 words**.

Question 2

You see this announcement in an English-language magazine.

> **Reading**
>
> What kinds of things do you enjoy reading?
>
> How enjoyable is it to talk about what you read with other people? Why?
>
> The best articles will be published next month!

Write your **article**.

Question 3

Your English teacher has asked you to write a story.

Your story must begin with this sentence.

Our new English teacher walked into the classroom and he didn't look happy.

Write your **story**.

Part 1

Questions 1 – 7

For each question, choose the correct answer.

---

1 Where does the girl want to go at the weekend?

A   B   C

2 When will the boy have his party?

A   B   C

3 Which photo does the woman like most?

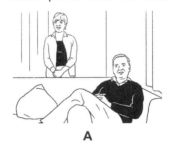 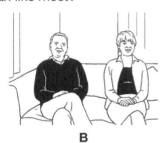 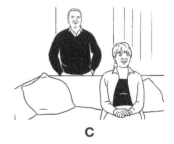

A   B   C

4 What will be on TV at 9 p.m.?

A   B   C

5   What do they decide to buy Ivan for his birthday?

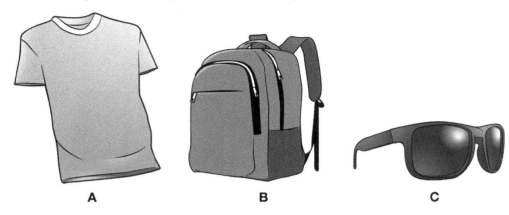

A   B   C

6   What time does the last bus leave?

A   B   C

7   What is the weather like today?

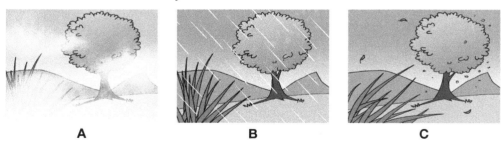

A   B   C

Questions 8 – 13

For each question, choose the correct answer.

---

8   You will hear two friends talking about fashion.
     What do they agree about?

   A   how expensive high-quality clothes are

   B   how important it is to be fashionable

   C   how good the latest fashions look

9   You will hear two friends talking about going climbing for the first time.
     How does the man feel about it?

   A   confident that he will be able to do it well

   B   satisfied that he will receive the right support

   C   excited about visiting a new area of the country

10   You will hear two colleagues talking about their jobs at a restaurant.
     What does the woman say about her job?

   A   There are some good rewards.

   B   It is interesting work.

   C   The social side is enjoyable.

11   You will hear a couple talking about their house.
     What do they say about it?

   A   It is becoming too small for what they want.

   B   It is starting to look better than it used to.

   C   It is in need of some small repairs.

12   You will hear two university students talking about some work.
     What is the girl trying to do?

   A   make the boy feel better about his result

   B   make a suggestion about working together

   C   make sure the boy understands a project

13   You will hear a brother and sister talking about a meal they have just had.
     What did they think about it?

   A   It was better than they expected.

   B   It included ingredients which were difficult to recognise.

   C   It is something they will try to make themselves.

Part 3

For each question, write the correct answer in the gap. Write **one** or **two words** or a **number** or a **date** or a **time**

You will hear a woman called Amanda Wright talking about holiday jobs for students.

Holiday jobs for students

There's a wide range of holiday jobs.

Most people decide to do a holiday job to get **(14)** ....

The best way to get information is from **(15)** ....

When applying for a job, make sure your letter is **(16)** ....

Prepare for the interview by doing **(17)** ....

Think carefully about what **(18)** .... are involved in a job.

Probably avoid jobs which are in the **(19)** ....

Questions 20 – 25

For each question, choose the correct answer.

You will hear a radio interview with a man called Jim Andrews about a steam railway.

20   Jim became interested in steam trains when

    A   he was at university.

    B   he visited his grandfather.

    C   he was given a toy train.

21   What does he currently do?

    A   He acts as chairman of the Steam Railway Club.

    B   He runs the Steam Railway Club website.

    C   He teaches train driving for the Steam Railway Club.

22   When did the original steam railway line close?

    A   1958

    B   1974

    C   1979

23   When did the Steam Railway Club take its first passengers?

    A   1995

    B   2000

    C   2003

24   What will the Club introduce next?

    A   educational visits for schools

    B   tickets to travel in the driver's section

    C   meals on the trains during journeys

25   What does Jim think is most important about the Club?

    A   bringing history to life

    B   making children interested in transport

    C   looking after trains and stations

Part 1 (2–3 minutes)

Phase 1

- What's your name?
- Where do you live?
- Do you work or are you a student?
- What do you do/study?

Phase 2

- Where would you like to go for your next holiday?
- What do you usually use the internet for?
- Tell me about your home.
- What do you usually talk about with your friends?

Part 2 (2–3 minutes)

4A Taking a selfie

Now, I'd like each of you to talk on your own about something.
I'm going to give each of you a photograph and I'd like you to talk about it.

A, here is your photograph. It shows **someone taking a selfie**.
[*Turn to photograph 4A on page 193.*]
B, you just listen.
A, please tell us what you can see in the photograph.

🕐 about 1 minute

Thank you.

4B Cycling

B, here is your photograph. It shows **people cycling**.
[*Turn to photograph 4B on page 197.*]
A, you just listen.
B, please tell us what you can see in the photograph.

🕐 about 1 minute

Thank you.

Part 3 (2–3 minutes)

Now, in this part of the test, you're going to talk about something together for about two minutes. I'm going to describe a situation to you.

[*Turn to the task on page 203.*]

A family want to spend a day out doing something together.

Here are some things they could do.

Talk together about the different things the family could do together and say which would be the most enjoyable for the whole family.

All right? Now, talk together.

 2–3 minutes

Thank you.

Part 4 (2–3 minutes)

- Where do you like going for a day out? Why?
- Do you prefer to go out in your free time or to stay at home? Why?
- How do you usually travel when you go for a day out? Why?
- Do you prefer going for a day out with friends or with your family? Why?
- Is it possible to have a good day out without spending much money? Why?/Why not?

 2–3 minutes

Thank you. That is the end of the test.

Part I

Questions 1 – 5

For each question, choose the correct answer.

___

1

NARROW TUNNEL

Cyclists – leave road and join pavement but look out for pedestrians!

A This tunnel is for cyclists and pedestrians only.

B Car drivers should look out for cyclists and pedestrians in the road.

C Pedestrians and cyclists should go through the tunnel on the pavement.

2

Debbie,
Brian's decided to attend the advanced guitar class and not the intermediate, and hopes you will too. Please let him know. It starts immediately after the intermediate class.
Vickie

A Brian wants Debbie to go to the same guitar class as him.

B Debbie should tell Brian the exact time his guitar class starts.

C Brian is asking to join the advanced guitar class that Debbie teaches.

3

TONIGHT'S PERFORMANCE

This window is only for collecting tickets you have paid for.

A This window is only for collecting tickets you have reserved.

B Remaining tickets for tonight's performance are on sale at this window.

C There are no more tickets available for tonight's performance.

4

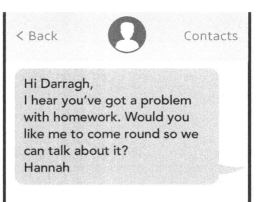

Hi Darragh,
I hear you've got a problem
with homework. Would you
like me to come round so we
can talk about it?
Hannah

A Hannah is asking Darragh to help her
with a problem.

B Hannah is offering to help Darragh
with a problem.

C Hannah is advising Darragh about
how to solve a problem.

5

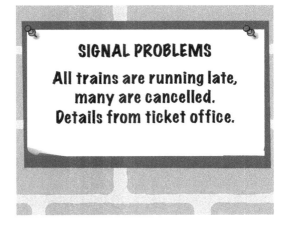

SIGNAL PROBLEMS

All trains are running late,
many are cancelled.
Details from ticket office.

A Because of signal problems, it is
impossible to travel by train at the
moment.

B Passengers should ask at the ticket
office whether the train they want is
running.

C The ticket office is currently unable
to provide information about the
times of trains.

Part 2

Questions 6 – 10

For each question, choose the correct answer.

___

The people below are all looking for somewhere to eat.

On page 99, there are advertisements for eight restaurants and cafés.

Decide which restaurant or café would be most suitable for the people below.

6  Juan is going to the cinema in the city centre and needs to eat after he finishes work at 5:30 p.m. He will have no more than an hour to eat. He loves steak.

7  Annie and Steve are going out for lunch to celebrate their wedding anniversary. They particularly like fish and want to go to a restaurant in an old building outside the city.

8  Fadel and some British friends are meeting at the stadium for an afternoon football match. He wants to introduce them to Middle Eastern food before the match starts. They are students, and can't afford much.

9  Tomiko and her friend Mafumi are visiting the city on Sunday and want to try some African food before they go to the art gallery in the afternoon.

10  Ebele has just finished college and her parents want to take her out on Saturday evening for a special dinner in the city centre. Ebele would prefer a restaurant that only serves vegetarian food.

Places to eat in and around the city

A   New Day

Since we opened forty years ago, thousands of people have come to taste what the Middle East has to offer. We're not far from the stadium and on bus routes from the city centre. You'll be surprised how little a good meal can cost! Open 9 a.m. till 4 p.m. every day.

B   Buckden's

Close to the art gallery, Buckden's offers wonderful steak at a price you can afford! Tell us if you're in a hurry and we'll serve you quickly. Open 12:30–5:30 p.m., Monday to Saturday.

C   The Red House

Whether or not it's a special occasion, come to The Red House. Situated in a seventeenth-century farmhouse in an attractive village within easy reach of the city, we've been open since 1990 and are famous for our fish and vegetarian dishes. Open seven days a week, noon until midnight.

D   Flamingo

Right in the heart of the city, beside the art gallery, Flamingo is the ideal vegetarian restaurant for a meal to remember. Our food is based on African recipes. Come for something quick before an evening out or spend the evening with us. Open every day except Sunday, 11 a.m. to 11 p.m.

E   Peggotty's

Just a short walk from the stadium, Peggotty's is a fish restaurant with a difference. Open every evening, we have live music and a great atmosphere. Our prices are very reasonable and if you eat with us this month, we'll give you a dessert absolutely free!

F   The Bridge

Eat at The Bridge and you'll want to come back soon – our customers say our steaks are the best in the world! And if you're short of time, don't worry – we'll make sure you leave when you need to. We're right in the centre of the city and are open from midday until late, seven days a week.

G   Riverside

For an affordable meal in a beautiful countryside location, come to Riverside. We serve traditional food and currently have a special offer on steaks: two meals for the price of one! We're open every evening from Wednesday to Sunday.

H   The Crocus

If you're looking for something special, look no further! Our menu offers you the best in food from all over Africa – meat, fish and vegetarian. The Crocus is close to the city art gallery and is open for lunch seven days a week.

Questions 11 – 15

For each question, choose the correct answer.

Clevedon Drama Club
by Warren Jackson

I've always lived in a town called Clevedon, in the UK. My parents love the theatre and my father writes plays in his spare time. He keeps sending them to publishers and though they always come back with a polite note saying 'No, thank you,' he never gives up. Still, a few drama clubs have performed his plays, so my first visit to the theatre was to see one of my father's plays being performed. As I was only eight, I was too young to understand it, so I didn't find it particularly interesting.

When I was sixteen, Clevedon Drama Club put on one of my father's plays. A week before the first night, however, there was a problem: the lighting designer fell ill. Nobody else in the club could take over, and my father asked me if I'd do it. I didn't really have time because of my high school work, nor did I have the required experience or knowledge. I can never say 'no' to a challenge, though, so I agreed and became a member of the club.

There was a lot of hard work for me to do before the first performance, just as there was for all those doing scenery, costumes and so on. But afterwards, I understood what a fantastic opportunity it had been, because I realised the difference good lighting can make to a show. It can attract the audience's attention, it can suggest danger, it can make the audience feel cheerful or relaxed. I found that so interesting! And after the shows, lots of people said the lighting was excellent!

Now I spend nearly all my free time at the drama club – apart from school, there's no time for anything else! I've designed the lighting for several productions and in the next one I'll be appearing on stage for the first time, which is amazing! It's only a small role, but it will make a change from painting scenery or selling programmes, which is what I usually do when I'm not doing the lighting. I still want to do that kind of thing in the future though, because it's fun and stress-free! It will help me in my chosen career, too – engineering.

11 What does Warren say about his father?

    A   He is a professional writer.

    B   He has had some of his plays published.

    C   He still hopes to achieve his ambitions as a writer.

    D   He is sometimes disappointed with performances of his plays.

12 Why did Warren join Clevedon Drama Club?

    A   He wanted to learn how they produced their shows.

    B   He was asked to help when they were in difficulty.

    C   He needed a change from his college work.

    D   He thought he could do the lighting well.

13 What did Warren enjoy about being involved in the production?

    A   working as part of a team

    B   preparing for the performances

    C   feeling that the lights were the best part of it

    D   learning how an atmosphere is created with lights

14 How does Warren feel about the next play the club is producing?

    A   proud of the work he's already done for it

    B   excited because he'll be acting in it

    C   glad he won't have to do boring jobs this time

    D   surprised he wasn't given a more important part

15 What would Warren's friends say about him?

    A

> He puts a lot of effort into the drama club. He'll never forget how successful he was when he first helped on a production there.

    B

> He's been keen on the theatre since he was a child, and would love to have a career in acting.

    C

> He and his father have similar interests. They're even planning to work together on plays in the future.

    D

> He thinks that drama is a good hobby because it helps with his studies. It's also very different from all his other hobbies.

Part 4

Questions 16 – 20

Five sentences have been removed from the text below.

For each question, choose the correct answer.

There are three extra sentences which you do not need to use.

Tennis

The sport of tennis has a long history. No one is quite sure when people first started playing something similar to the game we know today.

16 [ ] The ancient Egyptians, Romans and Greeks, for example, possibly all played a game using a ball and the palms of their hands. Historical documents show that around the year 1000, people in France were using their hands to hit a ball either over a rope or against a wall outdoors.

Over the next few hundred years a similar game became popular in many parts of Europe. The sport developed in various ways. For example, people stopped hitting the ball with just their hand. **17** [ ] This was eventually replaced by a piece of flat wood on a short stick, and wooden balls were replaced by lighter ones covered in leather. People also wanted to be able to play at all times of the year without getting wet. **18** [ ] Some of these are still in use today.

The game played on these courts was still very different from the sport that we now call tennis. Players scored points by hitting the ball with a racket into small windows covered by nets at the top of the court. There was also a net across the court, a bit similar to those used nowadays. **19** [ ]

During the nineteenth century, tennis balls started to be made of rubber and the game could then be played on grass. The new version of the sport was played in many different parts of the world, and the first Wimbledon tennis tournament was held in 1877 in London. **20** [ ] This rule changed a few years later. Since then, tennis has become one of the most widely played and watched sports in the world.

A   It was, however, much higher at the sides than in the middle.

B   They started to wear a glove instead.

C   These were already thousands of years old when they were discovered.

D   For instance, the best equipment available was a racket and a ball.

E   Only men were allowed to play in it.

F   Despite those problems, they soon attracted crowds of people.

G   It seems that it may actually have been a very long time ago.

H   As a result, a large number of indoor courts were built.

Part 5

Questions 21 – 26

For each question, choose the correct answer.

Bird-watching

The relationship between birds and human beings goes back a very long way – for thousands of years, in fact. Birds have always **(21)** .... us with food and feathers, but people have only been **(22)** .... in bird-watching since the late 1700s.

In the following century the study of birds became popular, although in those days it really only involved collecting birds' eggs. Rich collectors often **(23)** .... use of their contacts in other countries, asking for eggs and birds to be sent to them. By the end of the nineteenth century, people began to realise that birds needed to be **(24)** .... Many people became interested in watching living birds in their natural environment.

In the twentieth century, as cars became more **(25)** ...., bird-watchers started travelling around the countryside to look for birds they couldn't find in their own area. And in the 1960s, cheap air travel **(26)** .... people to go abroad to watch them.

21	A	provided	B	given	C	offered	D	delivered
22	A	curious	B	fond	C	keen	D	interested
23	A	made	B	got	C	put	D	took
24	A	kept	B	protected	C	held	D	reserved
25	A	average	B	regular	C	common	D	general
26	A	confirmed	B	encouraged	C	promised	D	supported

Part 6

Questions 27 – 32

For each question, write the correct answer.

Write **one** word for each gap.

Learning to play the violin

I've just started learning to play the violin. It's **(27)** .... of the most difficult

things I've ever tried to learn! Even after two months of lessons I still can't make a

sound with my instrument **(28)** .... doesn't hurt my ears. I don't know what my

teacher really feels because she just smiles and smiles. I don't know **(29)** ....

she can be so patient!

I hope that if I keep practising and having lessons, I'll finally start to improve. I

have **(30)** .... admit, however, that there are times when I think I should try a

different instrument. But I really love the sound of the violin when people play it well!

(31) .... I know I'll never be a very good player, I hope I'll finally **(32)** ....

able to play a simple tune one day!

Part 1

You **must** answer this question.

Write your answer in about **100 words**.

_____

Question 1

Read this email from your English-speaking friend Sam and the notes you have made.

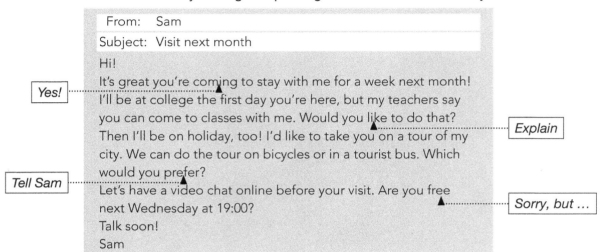

Yes!

From: Sam

Subject: Visit next month

Hi!

It's great you're coming to stay with me for a week next month!
I'll be at college the first day you're here, but my teachers say
you can come to classes with me. Would you like to do that?
Then I'll be on holiday, too! I'd like to take you on a tour of my
city. We can do the tour on bicycles or in a tourist bus. Which
would you prefer?
Let's have a video chat online before your visit. Are you free
next Wednesday at 19:00?
Talk soon!
Sam

Explain

Tell Sam

Sorry, but …

Write your **email** to Sam using **all the notes**.

Part 2

Choose **one** of these questions.

Write your answer in about **100 words**.

_____

Question 2

You see this announcement on an English-language website.

> **A useful job**
>
> What is the most useful job, in your opinion?
> Why is it so useful? Would you like to do that job?
> The best articles answering these questions will appear on our website!

Write your **article**.

Question 3

Your English teacher has asked you to write a story.

Your story must begin with this sentence.

As the woman got off the train, Jo saw that she had left her phone behind on the train seat.

Write your **story**.

Part I

Questions 1 – 7

For each question, choose the correct answer.

1 What will the weather be like tomorrow?

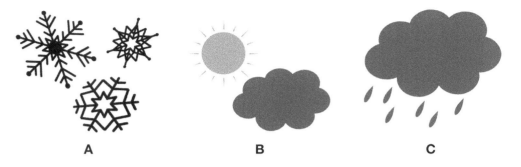

A   B   C

2 What class does Jessica decide to join?

A   B   C

3 What time did the man arrive home yesterday?

A   B   C

4   Which is the woman's flat?

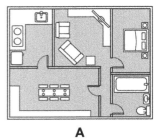 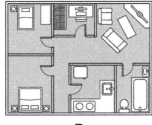 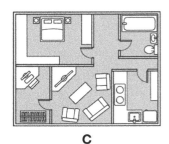

A   B   C

5   Where does Jill want Sally to go?

A   B   C

6   Which photograph are they looking at?

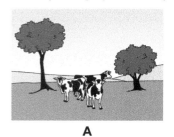 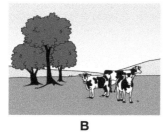 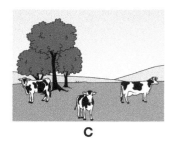

A   B   C

7   Where did the customer leave her glasses?

 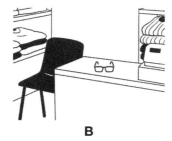 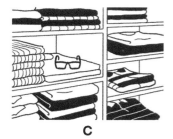

A   B   C

Questions 8 – 13

For each question, choose the correct answer.

___

8 You will hear two colleagues talking about their staff canteen.
What does the man dislike about it?

  A   It's noisy.

  B   It's crowded.

  C   It's expensive.

9 You will hear two friends talking about a dance class they both attend.
What does the woman say about it?

  A   The teacher is positive.

  B   The music is traditional.

  C   The other students are confident.

10 You will hear two friends talking about shopping.
What's the man doing?

  A   recommending a shop

  B   offering to buy something

  C   explaining a decision he made

11 You will hear a woman telling a friend about a swimming pool.
Why does she go there?

  A   The prices are low.

  B   The facilities are good.

  C   The location is convenient.

12 You will hear a brother and sister talking about a river trip.
How do they both feel about it?

  A   relieved it's over

  B   satisfied it was well planned

  C   surprised it was so enjoyable

13 You will hear two students talking about a teacher at their college.
What does the girl like most about him?

  A   He's kind.

  B   He's funny.

  C   He's clever.

Part 3

For each question, write the correct answer in the gap. Write **one** or **two words** or a **number** or a **date** or a **time**

You will hear a holiday representative talking to some new guests about their hotel.

Greville Weston Tours

Holiday representative: Cathy

This week's programme

Tomorrow: Free

Monday evening: Barbecue beside the **(14)** ....

                   Entertainment by teenage **(15)** ....

                   Starts at 8 p.m.

                   Sign the list before **(16)** .... p.m. on Monday

Wednesday morning: Coach trip to the **(17)** .... that can be seen in the distance

                   Take a **(18)** ....

                   Coach leaves at 9 a.m., returns around 4 p.m.

                   Cost of **(19)** .... is included

---

Questions 20 – 25

For each question, choose the correct answer.

You will hear a radio interview with a man called Jeremy about last weekend's television programmes.

20   What does Jeremy say about *Street Dancing*?

   A   It started late.

   B   It was cancelled.

   C   It was shorter than usual.

21   What did Jeremy particularly like about *Plants of Australia*?

   A   It was beautiful to look at.

   B   It gave a lot of information.

   C   It was filmed in unusual locations.

22   Jeremy says the series *Jojo's Party*

   A   ended at the weekend.

   B   will continue until October.

   C   started six months ago.

23   *Who Knows?* was different from usual because

   A   it was mostly about sport.

   B   it had a new group of experts.

   C   it included questions from the audience.

24   Jeremy thinks that Sunday's *Police Officer Briggs* was

   A   surprisingly good.

   B   the worst in the series.

   C   of its usual standard.

25   Vanessa Cosgrave wasn't in *It's Comedy Time!* on Sunday because

   A   she was away on holiday.

   B   she arrived late at the studio.

   C   she has left the programme.

Part 1 (2–3 minutes)

Phase 1

- What's your name?
- Where do you live?
- Do you work or are you a student?
- What do you do/study?

Phase 2

- When do you usually meet your friends?
- What do you usually do in the evenings?
- Tell me about your best friend.
- Tell me about the place where you live.

Part 2 (2–3 minutes)

5A Having a picnic

Now, I'd like each of you to talk on your own about something.
I'm going to give each of you a photograph and I'd like you to talk about it.

A, here is your photograph. It shows **people having a picnic**.
[*Turn to photograph 5A on page 194.*]
B, you just listen.
A, please tell us what you can see in the photograph.

🕐 about 1 minute

Thank you.

5B Working in an office

B, here is your photograph. It shows **people working in an office**.
[*Turn to photograph 5B on page 198.*]
A, you just listen.
B, please tell us what you can see in the photograph.

🕐 about 1 minute

Thank you.

Part 3 (2–3 minutes)

Now, in this part of the test, you're going to talk about something together for about two minutes. I'm going to describe a situation to you.

[*Turn to the task on page 204.*]

Two friends are going to travel together on a twelve-hour flight. They want to take something with them to do during the flight.

Here are some things they could take with them.

Talk together about the different things the friends could do together during the flight and say which would be the best.

All right? Now, talk together.

 2–3 minutes

Thank you.

Part 4 (2–3 minutes)

- What do you usually do on long journeys? Why?
- How do you prefer to travel on long journeys? Why?
- Which place in the world would you most like to visit? Why?
- Do you prefer to go on holiday with your family or with your friends? Why?
- Is it better to go on holiday in your country or in other countries? Why?

 2–3 minutes

Thank you. That is the end of the test.

Part 1

Questions 1 – 5

For each question, choose the correct answer.

1

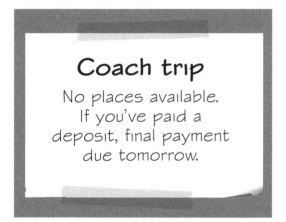

Tomorrow is the last day for

A paying what you owe for the coach trip.

B saying you want to go on the coach trip.

C paying a deposit for the coach trip.

2

A Kelly cannot collect any of the books she reserved until next month.

B Kelly can only keep the books she reserved for seven days.

C Kelly can now collect some of the books she reserved.

3

Once opened, the medicine in this bottle should be consumed within six months.

A You should drink the medicine in this bottle over a period of six months.

B You should drink the medicine no more than six months after opening the bottle.

C You should open this bottle within six months of buying it.

4

John,
I have to go out urgently, so I'm afraid you'll have to look after Belinda. Sorry you won't be able to go swimming after all.
Mum

This note asks John

A to take Belinda swimming with him.

B to go out with his mum instead of going swimming.

C to take care of Belinda instead of going swimming.

5

CHILDREN'S SCIENCE EXHIBITION

Machines have buttons which should be pressed to make them start.

A The machines are designed so that children can operate them.

B Children should be careful not to touch the machines.

C The machines are models which do not work.

Part 2

Questions 6 – 10

For each question, choose the correct answer.

The people below are all looking for somewhere to go on holiday.

On the opposite page, there are advertisements for eight holidays organised by the same company.

Decide which holiday would be most suitable for the people below.

6  Maggie would like a holiday with other people in their twenties. She wants to go diving during the day, and go out dancing and to different restaurants every evening. She only has a week free.

7  Marta and Alessia are interested in mountain climbing. They want to sleep in tents and make their own food, and to spend four or five weeks on their holiday.

8  Norbert lives in the countryside. He hopes to spend a few days in a big city, ideally in the home of somebody who can tell him about life in the city.

9  The Zhang family want to spend two or three weeks walking in the countryside. They would like to stay somewhere new each night, but don't want to have to carry their luggage.

10  Sonam and her parents want to go on holiday together for two weeks or longer. Sonam would like to explore different towns, but her parents would prefer to travel on a ship and relax on board.

Robson Clark Holidays

A Our guide leads a group of 12–15 people on a walk of around fifteen kilometres a day, through some of the most beautiful countryside in Italy. Each day's walk takes you to a different hotel, where you'll find your luggage has already arrived. Choose between tours lasting two and four weeks.

B Join a group of mostly young people for a lively holiday in a small town on a Greek island. Spend the day swimming, diving or sailing in the beautiful blue sea. There are plenty of places to eat and dance. Book any number of weeks, from one to four.

C Spend two weeks in New Zealand. You'll be based in a family hotel and our guide will lead walks through the amazing countryside with views of mountains in the distance. The hotel will provide picnic lunches, and there's dancing every evening!

D Cruise through the Great Lakes of North America and admire the wonderful scenery while you sit and relax on deck. Many of the towns where the ship calls have hardly changed for over a century. Each cruise lasts one week.

E We can help you visit some of the amazing sights of Peru. We've planned a route and can advise on where to camp and where to buy food. We can also supply tents and the essential equipment for mountain climbing. We recommend at least three weeks for this trip.

F Enjoy twenty-one days on a luxury cruise ship travelling from Cape Town to London. The ship offers a swimming pool, sports facilities, entertainment and five restaurants. And you can go ashore when it calls at ports along the coast of Southern and West Africa.

G Do you enjoy camping? Then this is the holiday for you! Three weeks in Sri Lanka based in a number of campsites with excellent facilities, where you can cook your own food or sample the fare prepared by experienced chefs.

H Learn about Mexico from its inhabitants! You stay as the guest of a Mexican family for up to a week – choose between a city and the countryside. You eat with them and they'll show you the places they like.

Part 3

Questions 11 – 15

For each question, choose the correct answer.

Working as a science journalist
by Shelly Langton

I work as a scientific journalist, writing articles about developments in science. I've always loved the subject and, having a degree in it, I know a lot about scientific theories and practices. My job is to make sure the public find out about the latest research. I'm one of the first people to find out from researchers about anything new and that's the best bit about what I do. The first time I saw my name on an article in a newspaper, it was amazing! I'm used to that now, though.

Writing can be challenging. Sometimes, scientists' work is very complex and there are ideas and technical words that I have to work hard to understand. Even more difficult is being able to explain things in a way that someone who isn't a scientist can understand. You need to develop a way of writing that's easy for people to follow when they read a newspaper. Getting the right title is also important, as that's what makes people want to read the article. I'm not bad at those things now.

If you work for a newspaper in their offices, you'll probably work from nine until five, which are normal office hours. I'm freelance, which means I write for different newspapers – thankfully, in the comfort of my own home. Often, articles have to be written quickly, so they can be published straightaway. This means working late to get things done, or I might have to miss a social occasion to get something finished. I knew that was part of the job when I started and it's fine because there are also times when I have nothing to write, and I can take a day off in the middle of the week.

There are opportunities to do fascinating things in science writing. Friends always seem surprised when I say I'm flying abroad to talk to a scientist. But things happen all over the world. I'm attending a conference in Germany soon, which I'm pretty excited about as I haven't been to one before. People often ask me if I work for science journals which scientists themselves read. I'm not qualified to do that and I prefer working for the popular media. You never know – one day that may change!

11 In the first paragraph, what does Shelly say she finds exciting about her job?

   A   seeing her name printed on articles

   B   learning more about her favourite subject

   C   knowing about discoveries before the public does

   D   spending time with people who do useful research

12 In the second paragraph, Shelly says that the hardest thing about writing is

   A   using language anyone can understand.

   B   understanding complicated ideas.

   C   making an article interesting to read.

   D   matching the styles of different newspapers.

13 What does Shelly say about the hours she works?

   A   They don't give her any free time.

   B   They aren't as long as she expected.

   C   They change depending on what she has to do.

   D   They are similar to the hours many people work.

14 What is Shelly looking forward to in the future?

   A   starting to do some international travel

   B   going to an important science event

   C   working for a science magazine

   D   getting a science qualification

15 What would Shelly say to a friend about her work as a science journalist?

   A   I enjoy taking part in scientific experiments as it helps me understand more about science.

   B   I didn't study science at university, which can make my job quite challenging at times.

   C   I find that the newspaper I work for often expects me to go into the office at weekends.

   D   I get to do a wide variety of things in my job, which keeps it interesting for me.

Part 4

Questions 16 – 20

Five sentences have been removed from the text below.

For each question, choose the correct answer.

There are three extra sentences which you do not need to use.

Huntingdon

Huntingdon is a small British town about 100 kilometres north of London. It is situated in an area of low land beside the Great Ouse river. It was probably too wet for people to live there until the Romans ruled England 2000 years ago and constructed many roads. One of them, Ermine Street, runs from London in the south to York, in the north of England. **16** They did this because it was a good location and it was possible to travel around both by the Great Ouse and the road. The first document to mention Huntingdon was written around 1400 years ago.

One of Huntingdon's inhabitants wrote in the twelfth century that the town was an attractive place, with many beautiful buildings. It became very rich compared to other towns. **17** These could provide wood for fuel, buildings and fences.

In 1205, King John confirmed Huntingdon's right to hold a weekly market. This was a common way to raise money in the Middle Ages (between the fifth and fifteenth centuries), as towns had to pay to hold a market. **18** This also meant the town was busy on the days when markets were held. Huntingdon had several small guest houses where visiting traders could stay overnight.

To celebrate the area's rich history, Huntingdon and the local area started a history festival in 2018. **19** They attended many activities, which included talks, films and music. Many of these events were sold out, which the organisers were very pleased about.

The organisers are now hoping to hold a history festival every year or every two years. **20** This should bring many more visitors to this very interesting historical place.

A   It was the main place for trade at the time, so this made sense.

B   But the king was unable to stop this from happening.

C   This first event attracted over 5000 people.

D   They were later destroyed because of this.

E   This was because it was surrounded by forests.

F   Of course, not many people were able to do things like that.

G   The main thing they want to do is to get people to know about it.

H   People began to build homes where it crossed the river.

Part 5

For each question, choose the correct answer.

My life in books

Like many people, it was my parents who taught me to read. I can't remember my life before reading, without books. When I started reading, a book was **(21)** .... pictures with only a few words. Now that I'm older, a book **(22)** .... only words in most cases. But I also love art books, and enjoy **(23)** .... the pages and looking at the beautiful pictures of famous paintings and statues.

I spend hours and hours reading, lost in other worlds, **(24)** .... all the people and places mentioned and what they look like. I may never experience things that happen in books **(25)** .... , but they are very interesting to read about.

I've never understood it when people **(26)** .... me that they don't enjoy reading. There are so many different things to read, from newspapers and magazines to novels and biographies, that there must be something they would enjoy!

21	A	approximately	B	completely	C	mainly	D	totally
22	A	requires	B	holds	C	keeps	D	contains
23	A	changing	B	turning	C	putting	D	placing
24	A	creating	B	dreaming	C	imagining	D	thinking
25	A	absolutely	B	directly	C	certainly	D	definitely
26	A	tell	B	say	C	confirm	D	advise

Part 6

Questions 27 – 32

For each question, write the correct answer.

Write **one** word for each gap.

Why I love street dance

I've been doing street dance for three years and I think it's a
great way to keep fit and have fun. You don't need any special
equipment other than comfortable clothes and trainers. All you
need **(27)** .... get started is the right music, love for dance,
(28) .... big enough space to move around in and loads of
energy! There's no need to go to classes either – I taught myself
from some brilliant videos online **(29)** .... showed me some
of the main moves, but I create my own moves **(30)** .... well.

Street dance is perfect for people **(31)** .... me who enjoy
dancing but don't want to follow a strict set of rules. There are
some very popular moves in street dance, such as 'pop-n-lock'
steps and 'krumping', but it's a really free kind of dance, so you
(32) .... even invent your own style. It's cool!

Part 1

You **must** answer this question.

Write your answer in about **100 words**.

Question 1

Read this email from your English-speaking friend Lee and the notes you have made.

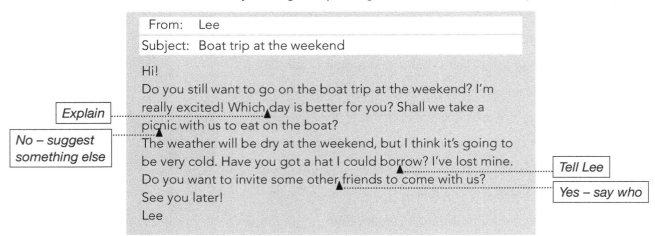

From: Lee

Subject: Boat trip at the weekend

Hi!
Do you still want to go on the boat trip at the weekend? I'm really excited! Which day is better for you? Shall we take a picnic with us to eat on the boat?
The weather will be dry at the weekend, but I think it's going to be very cold. Have you got a hat I could borrow? I've lost mine.
Do you want to invite some other friends to come with us?
See you later!
Lee

Explain

No – suggest something else

Tell Lee

Yes – say who

Write your **email** to Lee using **all the notes**.

Part 2

Choose **one** of these questions.

Write your answer in about **100 words**.

Question 2

You see this announcement in an English-language magazine.

Shopping

How much do you enjoy shopping and why?

Is it better to go shopping alone or with other people?

Where are the best places to shop?

The best articles will be published next month!

Write your **article**.

Question 3

Your English teacher has asked you to write a story.

Your story must begin with this sentence.

Pete picked up the expensive glass bowl to look at it more carefully.

Write your **story**.

Questions 1 – 7

For each question, choose the correct answer.

---

1   Where does Oliver want to work?

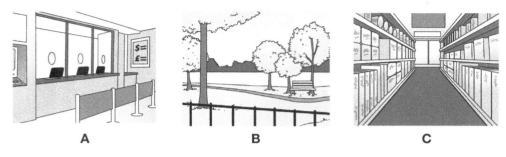

A   B   C

2   What will the man take back to the shop?

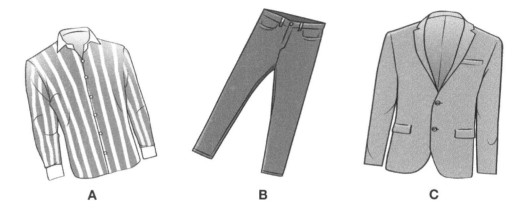

A   B   C

3   What event is the woman advertising?

A   B   C

4 Which performance did the man go to?

A

B

C

5 What is Jill going to talk about?

A

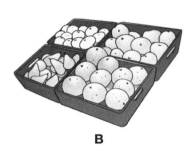

B

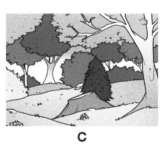

C

6 What will the woman take to the party?

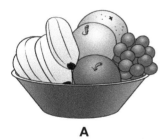

A

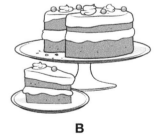

B

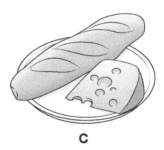

C

7 What does the boy spend most time doing?

A

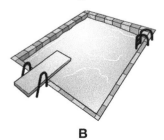

B

C

Part 2

Questions 8 – 13

For each question, choose the correct answer.

___

8   You will hear two friends talking about a cruise one of them has been on.
    How does the woman feel about the cruise?

   A   disappointed that it didn't last very long

   B   surprised by the limited range of shows

   C   delighted that she met so many people

9   You will hear two friends talking about the restaurant they are at.
    What do they both think of the food?

   A   There is too much of it.

   B   It should have more flavour.

   C   The variety of dishes is interesting.

10   You will hear a couple talking about decorating their house.
    What do they agree about?

   A   how long it will take to do

   B   how good it will look

   C   how expensive it will be

11   You will hear two students talking about a university project.
    What is the boy's attitude towards it?

   A   It has become a challenge to complete.

   B   There is too much to prepare.

   C   He doesn't find it interesting.

12   You will hear two friends talking about a sailing event.
    What is the woman doing?

   A   encouraging her friend to take part in the event

   B   offering to help her friend with something

   C   apologising to her friend for changing an arrangement

13   You will hear a brother and sister talking about the shop they are in.
    What is the girl's opinion of the shop?

   A   The prices have increased too much recently.

   B   The staff should serve people more quickly.

   C   The displays do not show the products well.

Part 3

Questions 14 – 19

For each question, write the correct answer in the gap. Write **one** or **two words** or a **number** or a **date** or a **time**

You will hear a radio announcement about a town festival.

Hartfield Festival

Celebrating the fact that the town is at least **(14)** .... years old

Photography competition

Age 11 and under: subject is **(15)** ' .... '

Age 12–18: subject is 'Hartfield's **(16)** .... '

Adults (19 and over): subject is **(17)** ' .... '

Entry forms – download from festival website

Closing date for entries: **(18)** ....

Three prizes in each category

Winners announced on 20 July

Exhibition of all photos in the **(19)** .... , from August to December

---

Questions 20 – 25

For each question, choose the correct answer.

___

You will hear a radio interview with a woman called Holly, who runs a restaurant.

20   Why did Holly start working in Palmer's Pizzas?

    A   The owner asked her to help.

    B   She needed to earn some money.

    C   A friend suggested that she applied.

21   What didn't Holly like about Palmer's Pizzas?

    A   The work was very tiring.

    B   She couldn't choose the menu.

    C   Some of the customers were rude.

22   When Holly decided to open a restaurant, it took a long time to

    A   choose a suitable building.

    B   raise enough money.

    C   find suitable staff.

23   When Holly's restaurant opened, the best thing was said by

    A   a customer.

    B   a waiter.

    C   a cook.

24   Holly thinks the most important thing about a restaurant is

    A   keeping prices low.

    B   serving food of excellent quality.

    C   making the customers feel welcome.

25   Holly is planning to

    A   continue running only one restaurant.

    B   open several more restaurants.

    C   change to a different type of business.

Part 1 (2–3 minutes)

Phase 1

- What's your name?
- Where do you live?
- Do you work or are you a student?
- What do you do/study?

Phase 2

- What's the weather like where you live?
- Would you like to have a part-time job?
- Tell me about the place where you work or study.
- What did you do yesterday?

Part 2 (2–3 minutes)

6A Relaxing at home

Now, I'd like each of you to talk on your own about something.
I'm going to give each of you a photograph and I'd like you to talk about it.

A, here is your photograph. It shows **people relaxing at home**.
[*Turn to photograph 6A on page 194.*]
B, you just listen.
A, please tell us what you can see in the photograph.

🕐 about 1 minute

Thank you.

6B Doing exercise

B, here is your photograph. It shows **someone doing some exercise**.
[*Turn to photograph 6B on page 198.*]
A, you just listen.
B, please tell us what you can see in the photograph.

🕐 about 1 minute

Thank you.

Part 3 (2–3 minutes)

Now, in this part of the test, you're going to talk about something together for about two minutes. I'm going to describe a situation to you.

[*Turn to the task on page 205.*]

Two college students want to do an interesting job together during their summer holiday.

Here are some jobs they could do.

Talk together about the different jobs the students could do and say which would be the most interesting.

All right? Now, talk together.

 2–3 minutes

Thank you.

Part 4 (2–3 minutes)

- What job would you like to do in the future? Why?
- Would you prefer to work indoors or outdoors? Why?
- Is it better to work on your own or with lots of other people? Why?
- Would you like to have your own business? Why?/Why not?
- What's more important: having a job you enjoy or making a lot of money? Why?

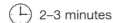 2–3 minutes

Thank you. That is the end of the test.

Part 1

Questions 1 – 5

For each question, choose the correct answer.

1

Claire is asking Jake

A how to get information about the camping trip.

B what she should take on the camping trip.

C when the camping trip is going to take place.

2

A The light comes on automatically when the train doors open.

B You can only open the train doors when the button is lit.

C If the light is on, the train doors cannot be opened.

3

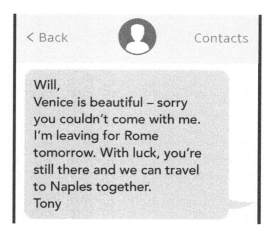

Tony hopes to meet Will in

A   Rome.

B   Naples.

C   Venice.

4

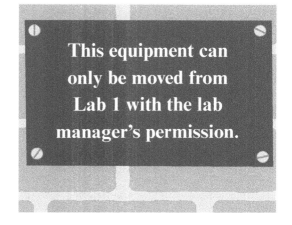

A   This equipment must only be used in Lab 1.

B   Ask the manager for permission before using this equipment.

C   Permission is unnecessary if you want to use the equipment in Lab 1.

5

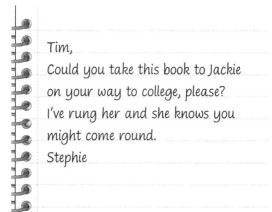

Stephie wants Tim to

A   collect a book from Jackie and give it to Stephie.

B   give Jackie a book when he is going to college.

C   phone Jackie and arrange to give her a book.

Part 2

Questions 6 – 10

For each question, choose the correct answer.

The people below all want to buy a book.

On the opposite page there are reviews of eight books.

Decide which book would be most suitable for the people below.

6  Valentina wants to become a writer and she enjoys reading any books which are by famous authors and are well written. She is very keen on books that make her use her imagination.

7  Loc is studying economics and he would like to read an exciting story where money plays an important part. He likes thrillers with plenty of action.

8  Lisa is training to become a teacher. She wants to understand what it was like to be a child in different countries in the past.

9  Shami wants a book that will help her to understand life for people who have moved to a different country. She would prefer fiction, ideally based on the writer's own experience.

10  Joe doesn't know much about science and would like to read a book that makes it easy to understand. He's particularly interested in the history of science.

Some of this month's new books

A *Work or Play*

We think we spend our time playing or at school – until we become adults. Diego Pireno reminds us that in earlier centuries, and in some places still today, millions of children had to work. He describes the lives of children around the world in the last two centuries.

B *The Money Book*

Before money was invented, people exchanged items or paid with anything that had a value for other people – such as shells or stones. Professor Joel Sandford explains how we started using coins and banknotes, and includes a number of surprising facts.

C *Room 74*

This is one of the best crime novels of the year. You won't be able to put the book down until you've reached the last page! An unlikely detective solves the mystery of a major bank robbery – but only after a series of exciting events and amazing surprises.

D *Running Wild*

Jane Terry is one of our most popular authors for children and normally writes very well. I am sorry to say, though, that her latest novel is a disappointment: a character's mother suddenly becomes her aunt, people appear in places that they couldn't possibly reach, and much more.

E *Why We Live As We Do*

Carol Conway has written several excellent books describing daily life in the last five centuries. In her latest, however, Conway explores how science has developed in the same period and its impact on people's lives – from electricity to plastic. People who know little or nothing about the subject will learn a lot from this book.

F *Ganjeera*

In *Ganjeera*, Karin Halvorsen creates strange and exciting pictures in the reader's mind, and the laws of science don't always operate. Halvorsen's skill at writing makes her one of the best-known and most popular novelists for young people – every word and every comma matters.

G *Mexican Adventure*

This is the latest in Gareth Young's long line of action novels and, as always, it's hard to guess what's going to happen next. Each of his novels is set in a different country. The characters of *Mexican Adventure* are footballers training for an international match.

H *Mountain Rose*

Akram Al-Djabri lived in Morocco until he was seven, when his father started working in Canada and the whole family soon followed him. Al-Djabri now lives in Germany. In this novel, the hero, Basri, leads a life that is very similar to Al-Djabri's.

Part 3

Questions 11 – 15

For each question, choose the correct answer.

Life as a hotel manager
by Kirsty Jenkins

I've always loved hotels. I never stayed in ones with gyms or spas on family holidays, but I loved the whole experience of not having to share a room with my sister. We never ate at hotels either, but went to cafés or had picnics. It was fun, though, and I always made friends with other guests my age.

Some hotels have hundreds of rooms, some just a few. You might think small hotels are friendlier, but making guests feel welcome isn't a question of size but attitude. Guests can be made to feel at home in a beautiful 900-room hotel with huge rooms, a swimming pool and prize-winning restaurants, and unwelcome in a hotel with a few bedrooms and just a small breakfast room. It all depends on the employees, from receptionists to cleaners to managers.

Many people start working in hotels because they enjoy meeting people and want to provide good service. My own reason was less interesting: I left university, my parents moved abroad and I had to get a job with accommodation. I went into the first hotel I saw and asked if they had any jobs. Luckily, a receptionist had left and I was offered the job – with a room in a separate part of the hotel where staff lived. We were all a similar age and got on well.

I decided to aim for hotel management. Ten years later, I'm running a twenty-room hotel in a city centre that was recently named 'Small Hotel of the Year' by a local tourist magazine. It isn't a luxury hotel, but it's great when guests tell you they've enjoyed their stay and hope to come back. We're offering a new menu soon and hope to attract more local people to our restaurant. Hotel staff often don't stay in their jobs long, for several reasons: students return to university, others do hotel work while they look for better-paid jobs, and sometimes they don't like the way the hotel is run. In the year I've been in charge, hardly anyone's left. Even some of the students have stayed on part-time. That's what makes me and the guests happy, and the future looks great!

11 How did Kirsty feel when she stayed in hotels as a child?

    A grateful to be able to spend time on her own

    B pleased about being able to try new food

    C delighted to watch guests come and go

    D excited about using the facilities

12 What does Kirsty consider most important for making guests enjoy their stay?

    A how experienced the managers are

    B how comfortable the rooms are

    C the variety of facilities available

    D the behaviour of staff

13 Kirsty started working in a hotel because

    A she wanted to work in a team with other people her age.

    B she was contacted by a hotel that was looking for staff.

    C she was trying to find work which included somewhere to live.

    D she wanted to gain experience of customer service.

14 In her present job, Kirsty is particularly proud that

    A many guests return to the hotel.

    B she has managed to keep people working there.

    C the hotel has won a national competition.

    D she has opened a successful hotel restaurant.

15 Which of these would Kirsty write to a friend?

    A
> After twenty years of working at the hotel, I finally feel like I know what I'm doing!

    B
> I'm glad I started working on reception because it gave me some great experience.

    C
> I love working in the countryside, but one day I'd like to manage a city-centre hotel.

    D
> It was so good to have all the support of my parents when I started working as a manager.

Part 4

Questions 16 – 20

Five sentences have been removed from the text below.

For each question, choose the correct answer.

There are three extra sentences which you do not need to use.

Book a cruise with us in the Baltic Sea!

The Baltic Sea is a fascinating area and the cities on its shores are among the most beautiful and historic in the world. **16** [ ] This means you can be sure of a starting date that suits you.

You will join your ship at Southampton, in the UK. **17** [ ] For example, you might visit Kiristiansand, in the south of Norway, a town with beaches, beautiful scenery and the Setesdal Vintage Railway. If trains are your thing, there'll be time for a three-hour ride on the railway, pulled by a steam engine over 100 years old.

Gothenburg, in the south of Sweden, has a modern opera house in the harbour, which was designed to look like a ship, and is a very popular venue. **18** [ ] But you may get the chance to see a show in Stockholm, where we stay overnight. Much of Sweden's capital is on islands, and you can travel between them by boat.

Copenhagen, the capital of Denmark, is famous for its statue of the Little Mermaid, a character in a children's story. **19** [ ] But there is plenty more to see in the city. Like Copenhagen, Helsinki, the Finnish capital, is small enough to explore on foot. Both cities are ideal for shopping, as they are famous for their contemporary design.

20 [ ] This city dates from 1703 and you will have two full days here, giving you plenty of time to admire the beautiful palaces, churches and other buildings. If you'd like a guided tour, there are plenty available – on foot, by car or by boat along the city's rivers and canals. Other tour stops include Tallinn, Riga and Oslo.

A   This is only a short distance from where you leave the ship.

B   This year we are offering more Baltic cruises than ever before.

C   When you are at sea, you will call at a number of exciting destinations.

D   There are many of these in the country, and visitors follow a route.

E   For many passengers, the best part of a cruise is a visit to the former Russian capital, St Petersburg.

F   You'll want to make this moment last as long as you can!

G   Don't be afraid to ask for advice about what to say.

H   Unfortunately, our visit will be too brief to attend a performance.

Part 5

Questions 21 – 26

For each question, choose the correct answer.

The skies above us

The weather has a huge effect on our lives. Consider the difference between waking up on a bright, sunny morning and waking up on a dark, wet morning. Don't you feel positive in the first **(21)** .... and maybe sad in the second? We use weather words to **(22)** .... about the way we feel: for example, if somebody **(23)** .... angry, we might say that their face 'clouds over'.

We do different things **(24)** .... on what the weather's like. How keen are you to go to the beach on a rainy day? We think about the weather before we select clothes to wear. Businesses are affected by weather, too. A company that produces ice cream, for example, must have enough to sell on hot days.

The weather even decides how your house is designed. If you live somewhere hot, it may be designed to **(25)** .... the heat out. If you don't, it's probably designed to **(26)** .... you from getting too cold.

21	**A**	point	**B**	time	**C**	case	**D**	fact
22	**A**	inform	**B**	tell	**C**	describe	**D**	talk
23	**A**	becomes	**B**	goes	**C**	makes	**D**	begins
24	**A**	basing	**B**	depending	**C**	following	**D**	deciding
25	**A**	continue	**B**	keep	**C**	contain	**D**	stay
26	**A**	miss	**B**	avoid	**C**	prevent	**D**	turn

Part 6

For each question, write the correct answer.

Write **one** word for each gap.

Longley's new shopping centre

I've lived in Longley all my life and there have been a lot of changes during that time.
The town centre **(27)** .... to be full of small individual shops, selling everything
you needed, from clothes and food to books and things for the home. It was a busy
place and people came to the town **(28)** .... surrounding villages to do their
shopping.

The new shopping centre has replaced the small shops, and this has brought
both benefits and disadvantages. The large supermarket has a **(29)** .... of
choice and opens late into **(30)** .... evening. There's a cinema and cafés, too,
(31) .... the town didn't have before. Unfortunately, the interesting little places
selling unusual or home-made items have gone and instead **(32)** .... those we
have the same boring chain stores found all over the country.

Part 1

You **must** answer this question.

Write your answer in about **100 words**.

Question 1

Read this email from your English-speaking friend Kim and the notes you have made.

From: Kim
Subject: Theatre show

Hi!
You asked me to check what's on at the theatre on Saturday.
There's a play about sailing, which sounds interesting, or a music
and dance show. Which would you prefer? There aren't many   *Explain*
seats left for either show. I can get them online tonight, if you like.   *Thank Kim*
Where shall we meet on Saturday?   *Suggest somewhere*
Do you want to do something after the show? We could have   *Sorry, but ...*
dinner.
See you soon!
Kim

Write your **email** to Kim using **all the notes**.

Part 2

Choose **one** of these questions.

Write your answer in about **100 words**.

Question 2

You see this announcement in an English-language magazine.

Articles wanted!

Special events

What's the best special event you've attended? Why was it so good?

Why do you think people like to celebrate special events?

We will publish the best articles next time!

Write your **article**.

Question 3

Your English teacher has asked you to write a story.

Your story must begin with this sentence.

When Hayley opened the box and saw a new camera inside, she was delighted.

Write your **story**.

Questions 1 – 7

For each question, choose the correct answer.

1   How does the man go home from work?

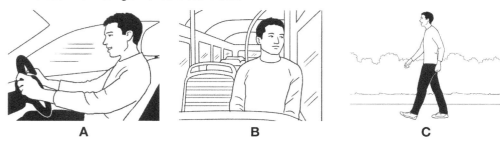

A   B   C

2   Who did Sophie go shopping with?

A   B   C

3   Who can callers see at the health centre today?

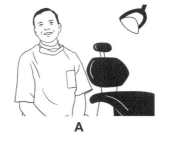

A   B   C

4 Which painting do they decide to buy?

A   B   C

5 Where is the man's computer now?

  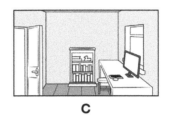

A   B   C

6 Which building will Carl take photographs of?

A   B   C

7 Why is the road closed?

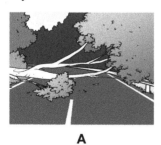  

A   B   C

Questions 8 – 13

For each question, choose the correct answer.

8   You will hear a boy telling a friend about a presentation he has to give at his college.
     How does he feel about it?

     A   unhappy about his choice of topic

     B   nervous about using equipment

     C   worried that he hasn't practised enough

9   You will hear two colleagues talking about their offices.
     What do they agree about?

     A   Only some of them should be painted.

     B   They should all be painted to look the same.

     C   None of them needs painting.

10   You will hear two friends talking about a TV quiz show.
     How does the woman feel about it?

     A   amused by the people taking part in it

     B   surprised by how hard the questions were

     C   disappointed that it wasn't more serious

11   You will hear two friends talking about a drama club they go to.
     What do they like best about it?

     A   the people they meet there

     B   the skills they learn there

     C   they things they discuss there

12   You will hear a woman telling a friend about a musical show she went to.
     What did she think of it?

     A   The music wasn't very well played.

     B   The jokes weren't particularly funny.

     C   The story wasn't realistic enough.

13   You will hear a man telling a friend about a department store.
     What impressed him about it?

     A   the attitude of the staff

     B   the range of things to buy

     C   the value for money

Part 3

Questions 14 – 19

For each question, write the correct answer in the gap. Write **one** or **two words** or a **number** or a **date** or a **time**

You will hear a woman talking to a group of young people about a youth club she helps to organise.

Spotlight Youth Club

Full-time youth worker: Caroline

More than 200 members

In two sections, open to people aged from 8 to **(14)** ....

Open:	Monday – Friday evenings and all day during weekends and school holidays
Sports activities:	**(15)** .... team has just won a competition
Art activities:	**(16)** .... is the most popular
Outdoor activities:	• next activity is **(17)** .... in Lake District
	• date: last weekend of **(18)** ....
Cost:	£65, including accommodation, food and transport by **(19)** ....

Questions 20 – 25

For each question, choose the correct answer.

You will hear a radio interview with a man called Paul Hammill about his city's spring festival.

20   What does Paul say about River Day?

   A   The public have requested more activities.

   B   People can join in some activities.

   C   Some of the activities are new.

21   On River Day, people will see

   A   sailing and motor boats.

   B   a boat race.

   C   copies of old boats.

22   Paul says that the five-kilometre Fun Run

   A   is limited to adults.

   B   is happening for the first time.

   C   is taking place in the morning.

23   For the sound and light show, people should start at

   A   the harbour.

   B   the city hall.

   C   the university.

24   The street market will include

   A   food from other countries.

   B   a variety of performers.

   C   activities for children.

25   How is this year's spring festival different from previous festivals?

   A   The cost of organising it is higher.

   B   It has taken longer to organise.

   C   More people helped to organise it.

Part 1 (2–3 minutes)

Phase 1

- What's your name?
- Where do you live?
- Do you work or are you a student?
- What do you do/study?

Phase 2

- What do you like about the area where you live?
- What do you think you will do tomorrow?
- Tell me about the things you like to read.
- What sports or games do you like to play or watch?

Part 2 (2–3 minutes)

7A Winter activities

Now, I'd like each of you to talk on your own about something.
I'm going to give each of you a photograph and I'd like you to talk about it.

A, here is your photograph. It shows **people doing a winter activity**.
[*Turn to photograph 7A on page 195.*]
B, you just listen.
A, please tell us what you can see in the photograph.

 about 1 minute

Thank you.

7B At a market

B, here is your photograph. It shows **someone at a market**.
[*Turn to photograph 7B on page 199.*]
A, you just listen.
B, please tell us what you can see in the photograph.

 about 1 minute

Thank you.

Part 3 (2–3 minutes)

Now, in this part of the test, you're going to talk about something together for about two minutes. I'm going to describe a situation to you.

[*Turn to the task on page 206.*]

A brother and sister would like to buy their parents a present to celebrate their thirtieth wedding anniversary.

Here are some things they could buy.

Talk together about the different presents the brother and sister could buy and say which would be the best.

All right? Now, talk together.

 2–3 minutes

Thank you.

Part 4 (2–3 minutes)

- Do you usually celebrate your birthday? Why?/Why not?
- What was the last big celebration you went to?
- Do you like going to celebrations with lots of people or only a few people? Why?
- Do you prefer going to celebrations with your friends or with your family? Why?
- Do you think people spend too much money on celebrations? Why?/Why not?

 2–3 minutes

Thank you. That is the end of the test.

Part 1

Questions 1 – 5

For each question, choose the correct answer.

1

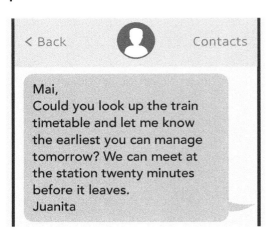

Mai,
Could you look up the train timetable and let me know the earliest you can manage tomorrow? We can meet at the station twenty minutes before it leaves.
Juanita

Mai should

A   contact Juanita after deciding what train they should catch tomorrow.

B   find out the time of the earliest train that runs tomorrow.

C   meet Juanita at the station so they can choose which train to catch.

2

No items of value are left in this shop outside opening hours.

A   No valuable objects are kept in this shop at any time.

B   Valuable objects are removed from the shop when it is closed.

C   If you leave any valuable objects in the shop, they will be kept safely.

3

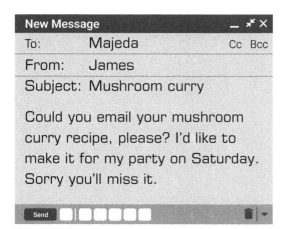

New Message

To: Majeda   Cc Bcc
From: James
Subject: Mushroom curry

Could you email your mushroom curry recipe, please? I'd like to make it for my party on Saturday. Sorry you'll miss it.

A   James is asking Majeda to help him cook some food on Saturday.

B   James wants to find out how to cook a mushroom curry.

C   James hopes that Majeda will be able to come to his party.

4

Touch screen to check in. Then wait for doctor to call your name.

A   Use this screen to let the doctor know that you have arrived.

B   Your name will appear on the screen when the doctor is ready for you.

C   Check that your appointment is shown in the list on the screen.

5

Roland,
Nick's train's due 6 p.m. but I can't get there. Could you meet him and take him to your place? I'll get there as soon as I can.
Karen

Karen hopes to see Nick

A   at her home.

B   at the train station.

C   at Roland's home.

Part 2

Questions 6 – 10

For each question, choose the correct answer.

The people below all want to do a course in their free time.

On page 153, there is information about eight courses in a college brochure.

Decide which course would be most suitable for the people below.

6  Aftab enjoys reading novels, plays and poetry in Arabic, French and English. He would like a course that uses his skills, and where he can study at home for a different number of hours each week.

7  Yuan spends all week sitting at a computer and she wants to do something physical and active on Saturdays. She would prefer an activity where she does something with other people.

8  Andries has never done anything creative and he would like to learn to paint. However, he works different hours each week, so he doesn't want a course at a fixed time.

9  Tina doesn't have a job. She likes making clothes for friends, cutting their hair and experimenting with make-up. She wants a course that will help her get a job where she can use these interests.

10  Mischa works at a sports centre but can take one day off each week to study. He would like to train for a new job where he can fix machines of some sort.

Calliston College: leisure courses

A Save money by learning how to repair your own car engine – or even qualify as a car mechanic. This is a course where you have plenty to do and very little to read. You'll learn how engines are made and have a lot of practice at repairing them. 9 a.m. until 4 p.m. every Tuesday.

B Join our Introduction to World Literature course! There's a weekly Wednesday evening class and instead of homework, we suggest books you can read in your own time – in the original language or in translation. So you decide how much time you spend reading each week.

C Are you afraid to use a computer? That can easily be changed! Join our computer class for beginners and you'll soon discover that it's much easier than you thought. Classes are held every day from Monday to Saturday, and you can come whichever day you like – and a different day each week, if you want to!

D Football for men and women! Even if you've never played before, come along on Monday evenings and have some fun. Ideal if you spend most of the day sitting down. We have several teams and there's sure to be one at the right level for you.

E Whether you're a beginner or advanced, you can study art at the college. You'll learn to draw and use oils. Instead of regular classes, one of our tutors will be available every day and evening, so you can come in when it's convenient for you.

F If you can spend the whole of every Thursday at the college, why not consider our fashion and beauty course? It prepares you for a range of careers, including hairdressing, fashion design and the theatre. Most employers will give you time off to attend.

G Have you ever thought about reading aloud? We run classes where you'll learn to read well and make new friends. Many of our students get work with a company that records both children's and adults' books.

H If you like being part of a team and want to do some exercise to keep fit, our swimming team is the perfect choice! It meets every Saturday morning and prepares for both competitions and displays. You don't have to be a good swimmer – we'll teach you if necessary.

Questions 11 – 15

For each question, choose the correct answer.

Walking for six weeks

My name's Anne and last summer my friend Lina and I walked for six weeks along the west coast of England. We'd done a two-week hike a year earlier and even though we'd found some of the walking quite difficult, we'd come back even better friends than when we'd left! On the first morning we couldn't believe we were on our way at last – our backpacks had been ready for weeks. We'd also talked to people who'd done the coastal walk, so we knew we could expect lots of adventures.

We weren't disappointed, although I hadn't done much exercise before our holiday and wasn't in great condition. The villages on our route were pretty, but it was the fantastic scenery that impressed us the most. Our accommodation in hostels was very basic, but we always slept well. I had a sore knee for a couple of days after slipping on a rock on a steep path, but it wasn't a big problem.

We never stayed anywhere for more than a night, apart from in one town with a beautiful castle. We arrived there late and were going to leave early the next day. But there was a terrible thunderstorm the following morning, and as the next part of our journey was along some high cliffs which some friends at home had warned us about, we thought we'd better not carry on that day. So we went on a tour of the castle instead and learnt all about life there over the centuries – and had a little break from hiking, too!

In another place, we chatted to a little girl whose family ran the hostel we were staying in. She wanted to know where we were from, what we were studying, what we wanted to do in the future, our favourite TV programmes – everything! She couldn't understand why so many people like walking because she preferred her bike. She thought it was very funny that Lina usually got to the top of every slope in about half the time it took me!

Now the trip is over, Lina and I agree it's one of the best things we've ever done. And we're already planning our next hike together!

11 How did Anne and Lina feel when they set off?

    A   pleased to be doing something new

    B   worried whether they would get on

    C   excited they had finally started

    D   nervous because of stories they had heard

12 What did Anne and Lina particularly like during their walk?

    A   the views they saw

    B   the meals they ate

    C   the beds they slept in

    D   the villages they walked through

13 Why did Anne and Lina stay an extra night in one place?

    A   They needed a rest.

    B   It had an interesting history.

    C   Some friends of theirs lived there.

    D   The weather was bad.

14 The little girl that Anne and Lina met was

    A   surprised by their plans.

    B   keen to offer them advice.

    C   curious about their lives.

    D   interested in doing a similar walk.

15 What message would Anne send to her family at the end of the walk?

A

> It's been really amazing! And you won't believe it, but I didn't have an accident during the whole of the trip!

B

> I must get fitter before my next walk! Lina was nearly always ahead of me when we were going up hills!

C

> Lina and I had a few arguments before we left. But in the end we both had a fantastic time!

D

> I can't wait to get back home and see you all again. I've missed my favourite TV programmes, too!

Part 4

Questions 16 – 20

Five sentences have been removed from the text below.

For each question, choose the correct answer.

There are three extra sentences which you do not need to use.

Scrabble

As a child, I loved playing *Scrabble*. It's a board game in which players are given seven letters each – on small flat pieces of plastic called 'tiles' – and take it in turns to make words, which they place on a board. Players score points depending on which letters they use and which squares they cover on the board. My family played it a lot and everyone was always very keen to win. **16** [ ] The only time most of it was worth knowing was during a *Scrabble* game, but that didn't matter to me.

When I was a teenager, I stopped playing for a few years. There was no particular reason for this. **17** [ ] Then one rainy weekend, my mother got the old *Scrabble* board out. My parents, my sister and I sat down to play and two hours later, the four of us were still round the table, arguing and laughing. **18** [ ] After that, I started playing a bit online and realised how popular the game is all over the world.

I preferred playing with people face-to-face, though, so I also began taking part in local *Scrabble* competitions. **19** [ ] For instance, there were only two players per board. Also, each player was timed, to make sure we each had the same number of minutes available to think during each game.

I did quite well and won a few prizes, but I knew I'd never be a world champion. Now I'm in my twenties, I'm too busy with work to be able to play regularly. **20** [ ] And when I visit my parents, we often get the board out and have a game together. I think that will always be my favourite way to play!

A   I couldn't believe I'd forgotten how enjoyable it was.

B   I didn't know any of the other players when I started.

C   I still enter competitions from time-to-time, but just for fun.

D   As a result, I learned some unusual vocabulary at an early age.

E   They take place every week, in a number of different locations.

F   However, these were very different from the family games I was used to.

G   I looked at the letters on my tiles and was very surprised.

H   I was just into other things, especially sport and computer games.

Part 5

For each question, choose the correct answer.

Bill Mackston

Bill Mackston's life today is very different from what it used to be. As a young boy, Bill always wanted to be rich. When he was still at school, he started small businesses: using equipment he borrowed from his father, for example, he **(21)** .... bikes that didn't work any more. He **(22)** .... his customers far less than the bike shop nearby.

After he left school, he **(23)** .... one company after another. And each one was more **(24)** .... than the last. He **(25)** .... thousands of people in several countries and owned seven houses, a helicopter, a plane, two boats and twenty cars.

But Bill was actually very lonely and never knew whether the people around him liked him or his money more. So one day he gave everything **(26)** .... He just stopped. Now he lives on a very small farm, where he grows vegetables and spends time with his friends.

21	A	fixed	B	turned	C	changed	D	managed
22	A	demanded	B	charged	C	asked	D	required
23	A	held	B	set	C	ran	D	put
24	A	successful	B	experienced	C	positive	D	qualified
25	A	earned	B	included	C	applied	D	employed
26	A	in	B	off	C	up	D	out

Part 6

Questions 27 – 32

For each question, write the correct answer.

Write **one** word for each gap.

My city

I live in Copenhagen and I love it! I think it's **(27)** .... great place to live
because it isn't too big, but it's still large enough to be interesting. Tourists can
easily visit most of the city on foot or they can travel around by bike, **(28)** ....
most of the people who live here. Almost everyone here cycles to school or work
every day.

There are lots of parks in my city too, as **(29)** .... as some great art galleries
and museums. In the summer, I go to the Tivoli gardens with my family. There are
beautiful plants and fountains, lots of great rides and even theatre shows.

(30) .... Copenhagen is by the sea, it's easy **(31)** .... me to go
swimming at a beach called Bellevue just north of the city. And near Bellevue
there's a big forest called Dyrehaven. I love going there **(32)** .... walk and take
photographs.

Part 1

You **must** answer this question.

Write your answer in about **100 words**.

Question 1

Read this email from your English-speaking friend Chris and the notes you have made.

| From: | Chris |
| Subject: | Bike ride |

Hi!
Do you still want to go for a long bike ride with me for two days next weekend?

Yes!

We'll be away for one night. Shall we take small tents to sleep in?

Tell Chris

We need to think about food during the trip, but I'm very busy at work at the moment. Could you help with this, please?

Offer to ...

You said your bike was quite old. Would you like to borrow my brother's for the trip?

Thanks, but ...

Let me know!
Chris

Write your **email** to Chris using **all the notes**.

Part 2

Choose **one** of these questions.

Write your answer in about **100 words**.

Question 2

You see this announcement on an English-language website.

Celebrations

What kind of things do families and friends celebrate together in your country?

Is there a celebration that you particularly enjoy? What happens at this celebration?

Why do you like it?

We'll publish the best articles answering these questions.

Write your **article**.

Question 3

Your English teacher has asked you to write a story.

Your story must begin with this sentence.

When Kevin arrived, everyone was really surprised to see him.

Write your **story**.

Part 1

Questions 1 – 7

For each question, choose the correct answer.

---

1 When will the youth orchestra's concert take place?

A   B   C

2 Where will the woman go on holiday?

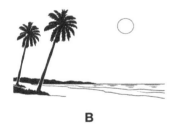

A   B   C

3 Where does the man live?

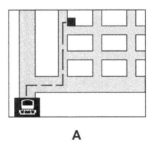
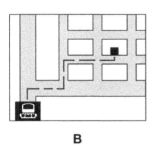
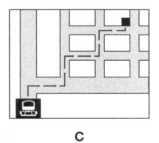

A   B   C

4 What has the man found?

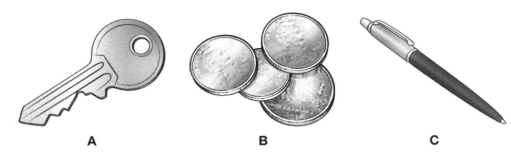

A   B   C

5 What is particularly cheap at the moment?

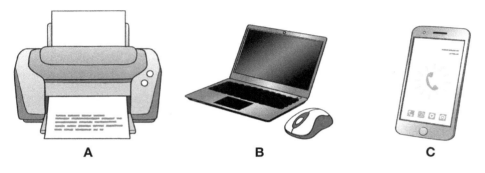

A   B   C

6 Where has the woman parked her car?

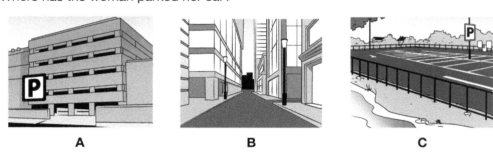

A   B   C

7 Where are they going to eat?

A   B   C

Questions 8 – 13

For each question, choose the correct answer.

---

8   You will hear two photographers talking about their work.
    What do they both find challenging?

    A   having problems with equipment

    B   seeing disappointed customers

    C   waiting for wildlife to appear

9   You will hear two friends talking about a dinner party they are having.
    How does the man feel about it?

    A   positive about how well the evening will go

    B   satisfied that he has prepared a good meal

    C   relieved that all his guests are able to attend

10 You will hear two friends talking about plans for a new leisure centre in their town.
    What does the woman think?

    A   It will be an attractive building.

    B   It will be expensive to use.

    C   It will be helpful for the town.

11 You will hear a brother and sister talking about a family holiday they are going on.
    What do they both agree?

    A   It will be fun to spend time together.

    B   It will be interesting to see somewhere new.

    C   It will be good to relax for a change.

12 You will hear a man talking to a woman about work.
    Why is he talking to her?

    A   to tell her about something he'd like to do

    B   to complain about something

    C   to get some advice

13 You will hear a woman telling her friend about a competition she has entered.
    What does she think about it?

    A   It will be fairly easy to win a prize.

    B   It is about an interesting topic.

    C   It may help her studies.

Part 3

For each question, write the correct answer in the gap. Write **one** or **two words** or a **number** or a **date** or a **time**

You will hear a teacher talking to some students about a shopping trip that he has organised for them.

Shopping trip to Burlington

The bus will wait at the **(14)** .... of the college.

The meeting time is **(15)** ....

One group will go with Zac to a **(16)** .... shop.

The second group will go to the city's largest **(17)** .... store.

Students should bring a packed lunch to eat at picnic tables at the **(18)** ....

Departure time is 4:00 p.m. from the bus station on **(19)** ....

Questions 20 – 25

For each question, choose the correct answer.

You will hear a radio interview with a woman called Gwen about her work as an actor.

20 Why did Gwen want to become an actor?

    A   She enjoyed being the centre of attention.

    B   She wanted to meet famous actors.

    C   She liked the atmosphere in the theatre.

21 Gwen was first paid as an actor

    A   when she was a child.

    B   when she was at drama college.

    C   when she joined a theatre company.

22 Gwen is most interested in roles that are

    A   very different from her.

    B   similar to people she knows.

    C   the sort of person she would like to be.

23 Gwen says that people who want to be actors should definitely

    A   pay attention to human behaviour.

    B   read as many plays as possible.

    C   see a range of shows at the theatre.

24 Gwen is now working on a play by

    A   a friend of hers.

    B   a famous actor.

    C   an unknown writer.

25 Gwen is helping a student production by

    A   acting in the play.

    B   directing the actors.

    C   encouraging people to attend the play.

Part 1 (2–3 minutes)

Phase 1

- What's your name?
- Where do you live?
- Do you work or are you a student?
- What do you do/study?

Phase 2

- Why are you learning English?
- Where do you usually meet your friends?
- How often do you eat out at restaurants?
- Tell me about the TV programmes or films you like to watch.

Part 2 (2–3 minutes)

8A In a café

Now, I'd like each of you to talk on your own about something.
I'm going to give each of you a photograph and I'd like you to talk about it.

A, here is your photograph. It shows **people spending time in a café**.
[*Turn to photograph 8A on page 195.*]

B, you just listen.

A, please tell us what you can see in the photograph.

🕐 about 1 minute

Thank you.

8B Shopping for clothes

B, here is your photograph. It shows **people choosing clothes**.
[*Turn to photograph 8B on page 199.*]

A, you just listen.

B, please tell us what you can see in the photograph.

🕐 about 1 minute

Thank you.

Part 3 (2–3 minutes)

Now, in this part of the test, you're going to talk about something together for about two minutes. I'm going to describe a situation to you.

[*Turn to the task on page 207.*]

A couple with a young child want to go away on holiday for two weeks.

Here are some places they could go.

Talk together about the different places they could go and say which would be the best for the whole family.

All right? Now talk together.

 2–3 minutes

Thank you.

Part 4 (2–3 minutes)

- Where did you stay on your last holiday? Why?
- Is it better to have a holiday with your family or with friends? Why?
- Do you prefer visiting hot countries or cold countries on holiday? Why?
- Is it nice to stay at home sometimes when you have holiday from work/college/ school? Why?/Why not?
- Do you think students get too much time off school or college? Why?/Why not?

 2–3 minutes

Thank you. That is the end of the test.

GRAMMAR BANK

Present simple

Positive

I/We/You/They	know.
He/She/It	know**s**.

Negative

I/We/You/They	**don't** know.
He/She/It	**doesn't** know.

Questions

Do	I/we/you/they	know?
Does	he/she/it	

Short answers

Yes,	I/we/you/they	**do**.
	he/she/it	**does**.
No,	I/we/you/they	**don't**.
	he/she/it	**doesn't**.

We use the present simple to talk about:

- permanent states.
  *He **lives** in America.*

- habits or repeated actions.
  *She **visits** her parents most weekends.*

Present continuous

Positive

I	**'m (am)**	talk**ing**.
He/She/It	**'s (is)**	
We/You/They	**'re (are)**	

Negative

I	**'m not (am not)**	talk**ing**.
He/She/It	**isn't (is not)**	
We/You/They	**aren't (are not)**	

Questions

Am	I	talk**ing**?
Is	he/she/it	
Are	we/you/they	

Short answers

Yes,	I	**am**.
	he/she/it	**is**.
	we/you/they	**are**.
No,	I	**'m not**.
	he/she/it	**isn't**.
	we/you/they	**aren't**.

We use the present continuous to talk about:

- actions that are happening now.
  *He**'s making** dinner.*

- actions that are happening around now.
  *We**'re learning** to ski.*

Note: Look at the spelling changes:
*cut – cutting   mak**e** – mak**ing***

Present simple and Present continuous

We can contrast permanent activities (present simple) with activities happening now, today or around this time (present continuous).
*I**'m working** in Greece this summer but I **live** in Newcastle.*

Practice

1   Choose the correct verb forms to complete the email.

> **New Message**
>
> Hi Helga,
>
> Thanks for your email. Let me tell you a few things about myself.
>
> I'm nineteen and I **(a)** *study / 'm studying* English Literature at college. I'm originally from London, but at the moment I **(b)** *stay / 'm staying* at my grandparents' house because it's nearer my college, in Cambridge. I **(c)** *look for / 'm looking for* a place of my own, which I'm going to share with two of my friends from college. I **(d)** *usually go out / 'm usually going out* with friends at weekends but today I **(e)** *watch / 'm watching* TV at home because it **(f)** *snows / 's snowing*. What about you? **(g)** *Does it often snow / Is it often snowing* in Oslo? What **(h)** *do you do / are you doing* when it snows?
>
> Write soon,
>
> Rory

Stative verbs

Stative verbs describe states, not actions. We don't usually use them in the continuous form. Some common stative verbs are:

- verbs of being and owning, e.g. *be*, *have*, *own*
- verbs of feeling or wanting, e.g. *hate*, *like*, *love*, *need*, *prefer*, *want*, *wish*
- verbs of thinking, e.g. *agree*, *believe*, *know*, *remember*, *think*, *understand*
- verbs that describe the senses, e.g. *feel*, *hear*, *smell*, *see*, *taste*
- verbs that describe appearance and qualities, e.g. *appear*, *look* (= seem), *seem*, *sound*
- other verbs, e.g. *cost*, *mean*.

Note: We can use some stative verbs in the continuous form when we describe actions, but the meaning is different.

*He's **having** breakfast at the moment.* (having = eating)

*We're **thinking** about moving house.* (thinking = considering)

Practice

1 **Choose the correct words to complete the sentences.**

   a *Do you like / Are you liking* Japanese music?

   b My father *doesn't know / isn't knowing* how to cook.

   c *Are you thinking / Do you think* it will rain later?

   d We *have / 're having* a meal. Do you want to join us?

   e Are you *seeing / looking at* the photos on your phone?

   f Jill's *listening to / hearing* music in her room.

Adverbs of frequency, time phrases

We use adverbs of frequency to say how often something happens. Some common adverbs of frequency are: *always*, *usually*, *frequently*, *often*, *sometimes*, *occasionally*, *rarely*, *hardly ever*, *never*.

Adverbs of frequency come:

- before main verbs.
  *I **never watch** TV.*
- after *be*.
  *Harry **is always** late.*

- after auxiliary and modal verbs.
  *He **doesn't usually** get up early on Sundays.*
  *You **must never** swim at this beach.*

Other time expressions usually go at the end of a sentence.

*The team practises **twice a week.***

Practice

1 **Write these words and phrases in the correct place in the table.**

at the moment   every day   never
now   often   on Fridays   once a year
this week   today   usually

present simple	present continuous

2 **Choose six words or phrases from Exercise 1. Use them to write true sentences about you.**

Past simple

Positive

I/He/She/It/We/You/They	**watched** the film.

Negative

I/He/She/It/We/You/They	**didn't watch** the film.

Questions

Did	I/he/she/it/we/you/they	**watch** the film?

Short answers

Yes,	I/he/she/it/we/you/they	**did**.
No,	I/he/she/it/we/you/they	**didn't**.

We use the past simple to talk about:

- an action that started and finished in the past.
  *Kyle **walked** home.*
- two or more past actions that happened one after the other.
  *I **had** lunch and then **watched** TV.*
- a past habit or regular past event.
  *My brother **worked** hard all year.*

Note: Look at the spelling changes:

*look – look**ed**   cure – cur**ed**   study – stud**ied***
*sho**p** – sho**pped***

Past continuous

Positive

I/He/She/It	**was**	talk**ing**.
We/You/They	**were**	

Negative

I/He/She/It	**wasn't**	talk**ing**.
We/You/They	**weren't**	

Questions

Was	I/he/she/it	talk**ing**?
Were	we/you/they	

Short answers

Yes,	I/he/she/it	**was**.
	we/you/they	**were**.
No,	I/he/she/it	**wasn't**.
	we/you/they	**weren't**.

We use the past continuous to:

* talk about an action in progress in the past.
  *I **was listening** to music.*
  *We **were cooking** a meal.*

* set the scene in a story.
  *The sun **was shining**.*
  *We **were waiting** for our friends.*

We use the past simple for an action that interrupts or happens during another action in progress in the past. For the action in progress, we use the past continuous.

*Ella **was living** in Hong Kong when she **met** Lee.*

We can use *while* instead of *when*, but we put *while* before the past continuous verb.

*The phone rang **while** I **was watching** a film.*
***When** the phone rang, I **was watching** a film.*

Practice

1 **Complete the sentences with the past simple form of the verbs in brackets.**

a Where .... (be) James yesterday?

b We .... (enjoy) the book more than the film.

c The play .... (not start) on time.

d I .... (see) Kevin last week.

e We .... (practise) every day for a month.

f The children .... (not want) to go out in the rain.

2 **Complete the sentences with the past continuous form of the verbs in brackets.**

a What .... (you/do) at this time last week?

b I .... (not live) in Hungary last year.

c .... (you/play) football when the teacher arrived?

d The internet .... (not work) yesterday, so we couldn't go online.

e Was the weather nice while .... (you/walk) yesterday?

f The television was on, but Sam .... (not pay) attention to it.

–ing form

We use the *–ing* form:

* as the subject or object of a sentence.
  ***Eating** vegetables is good for you.*
  *He really loves **surfing**!*

* after prepositions.
  *I always end **up leaving** my keys at home.*
  *We went home **after finishing** our game.*

* after some verbs: *begin, continue, enjoy, finish, hate, like, love, imagine, practise, remember, start, stop, suggest.*
  *I can't **imagine living** without music.*
  *I **remember stopping** at the shop on the way home.*

Practice

1 **Complete the sentence with the correct form of these verbs.**

eat	give	look	paint	swim	think

a .... is probably the best form of exercise.

b Michael doesn't like .... presentations at college. He's very shy.

c My cousin didn't want to go to the zoo – she's not interested in .... at animals.

d After .... my lunch, I went round my friend's house.

GRAMMAR BANK

e Without _____, Claire ran into the garden and rescued the bird.

f My dad finished _____ the bedroom yesterday. It looks great!

Will

Positive

I/He/She/It/We/You/They	'll (will)	win.

Negative

I/He/She/It/We/You/They	won't (will not)	win.

Questions

Will	I/he/she/it/we/you/they	win?

Short answers

Yes,	I/he/she/it/we/you/they	will.
No,	I/he/she/it/we/you/they	won't.

We use *will*:

- to talk about our personal ideas and opinions about the future.
  *Perhaps we **will use** e-books for all our studies in the future.*

- to make offers.
  *I**'ll help** you with that bag.*

- for unplanned decisions that we make at the time we are speaking.
  *I feel tired. I think I**'ll go** home now.*

Going to

Positive

I	'm (am)	going to	leave.
He/She/It	's (is)		
We/You/They	're (are)		

Negative

I	'm (am) not	going to	leave.
He/She/It	isn't (is not)		
We/You/They	aren't (are not)		

Questions

Am	I	going to	leave?
Is	he/she/it		
Are	we/you/they		

Short answers

Yes,	I	am.
	he/she/it	is.
	we/you/they	are.
No,	I	'm not.
	he/she/it	isn't.
	we/you/they	aren't.

We use *going to* to talk about:

- intentions and plans for the future that haven't been arranged or agreed yet.
  *I**'m going to visit** my friend in Turkey sometime next year.*

- things that we expect to happen because of outside information.
  *It**'s going to rain** soon.* (There are big grey clouds.)

Present continuous and Present simple

We use the present continuous for future arrangements. These are activities that we've agreed to do with other people. We know the details such as when, where, etc.
*I**'m having** lunch with Sarah on Saturday.*

We use the present simple for schedules and timetabled events.
*The film **finishes** at 9:30 p.m.*

Practice

1 **Find and correct the mistakes with future forms in six of the sentences.**

a Oh look, there's no bread left. I'm going to the shop to get some.

b My friends go to the cinema later.

c I'm not sure why but I think the match tomorrow is being exciting.

d Do we play tennis after work?

e Ella's going to start school next year.

f Matt's listening to music later.

g The class starts at five on Friday.

h What time is the train leaving?

2 **Complete the sentences with the most appropriate future form of the verbs in brackets.**

a I .... (meet) Sandra at the theatre in ten minutes.

b I think Martin .... (be) tired tonight. He's been busy all day.

c The train .... (leave) at 2 p.m., so we've got an hour to get there.

d Verity .... (come) to visit me next week.

e Watch out! The dog .... (jump) on you!

f That suitcase looks too heavy for you! I .... (take) it upstairs.

g Where .... (you/meet) Joe tomorrow?

h The film .... (start) at 8:00 p.m., so don't be late.

Advice

We use *should/shouldn't* + infinitive to give advice. This is an opinion about what we think is a good or bad idea.
*You **should have** a nap. You look tired.*
*You **shouldn't drive** so fast.*

We use *should* in questions to ask for advice.
*What **should I do**?*
*Where **should** we **go** to get the bus?*

Suggestions

We use *how about* + noun/–ing, *why don't you/ we* + infinitive and *you could* + infinitive to make a suggestion. This is an idea for the listener to consider. We use *you could* + infinitive when different options are possible.
How about watching a film?
Why don't we go out?
We could go by train or we could cycle.

We use *shall I/we* + infinitive for suggestions and offers.
***Shall I bring** some crisps for the picnic?*
*What **shall we do** after work today?*

Practice

1 **Complete the conversation with one word in each gap.**

A: **(a)** .... we start making our video today?

B: Yeah, our presentation is next week – we don't have much time.

A: We **(b)** .... film young people doing different activities in their free time.

B: Good idea. **(c)** .... don't we go to the skate park and film there?

A: All they do there is skateboard. We **(d)** .... go somewhere different and film as many different activities as possible.

B: Alright. How **(e)** .... the park? People do all sorts of activities there.

A: Sounds good. Shall **(f)** .... message Leanne and see if she wants to join us?

B: OK … Done!

Present perfect

Positive

I/We/You/They	've (have)	started.
He/She/It	's (has)	

Negative

I/We/You/They	haven't (have not)	started.
He/She/It	hasn't (has not)	

Questions

Have	I/we/you/they	started?
Has	he/she/it	

Short answers

Yes,	I/we/you/they	have.
	he/she/it	has.
No,	I/we/you/they	haven't.
	he/she/it	hasn't.

We use the present perfect simple to talk about:

• something that happened at an unspecified time in the past.
*Sarah and I **have met** before.*

- experiences.
  She's climbed Mount Kilimanjaro.
- something that happened in the past and has a result in the present.
  That player has broken his leg, so he can't play.
- a situation or an experience in our lives that is still true now.
  I've lived in this town all my life.

Present perfect with adverbs of time

We use *ever* in questions and statements to talk about whether an event or experience happened/ didn't happen at some point in the past.
Have you ever lived in another country?

We use *never* to talk about something that hasn't happened.
I've never eaten Korean food.

We use *yet* in negative statements and questions to say whether something that was expected has happened.
I haven't finished my homework yet.
Has she found a job yet?

We use *just* for recent events.
I've just had a text from my friend.

We use *already* for something that has happened before now.
We're not hungry because we've already had lunch.

We often use *for* and *since* with the present perfect.
I haven't heard this song for years. (a period of time)
I've known Ian since I was seven. (a specific time in the past)

Practice

1   Complete the sentences with the present perfect form of the verbs in brackets.

   a   We .... (buy) a ticket for the festival.

   b   He .... (not read) my email yet.

   c   Emily .... (not eat) Chinese food before.

   d   Which of these activities .... (you/try)?

   e   How long .... (he/be) at this college?

2   Complete the sentences with *ever*, *never*, *yet*, *just* or *already*.

   a   Have you .... had a job interview?

   b   I've .... been to India. I'd love to go one day.

   c   Lindi, have you found your phone .... ?

   d   Tyler didn't want to see the film because he's .... seen it.

   e   We've .... bought some food for this evening. We got it a few minutes ago.

Past simple and Present perfect

We use the past simple for an action that happened at a definite time in the past.
I joined a chess club a few weeks ago.

We use the present perfect simple for a past action when we don't know when it happened, or when it isn't important.
We've visited this town before.

We also use the present perfect for something that happened in the past but in a period of time that is not finished, e.g. *today, this month*.
I've made a lot of new friends this year.

Practice

1   Complete the conversation with the past simple or present perfect form of the verbs in brackets.

   A: Everyone at college was talking about our video about freerunning this morning.

   B: Yeah, Lisa **(a)** .... (text) me a few minutes ago. She says 250 people **(b)** .... (watch) it already. That's brilliant for the first day.

   A: I think we **(c)** .... (do) really well, don't you?

   B: Yes, it was a good idea. So lots of people **(d)** .... (see) the video. Do you think they liked it?

   A: Definitely! They **(e)** .... (leave) some really good comments. I think that before we **(f)** .... (make) the video, a lot of people at college had the wrong idea about freerunning. They **(g)** .... (not think) it was a real sport.

   B: That's right. And now the video **(h)** .... (show) everyone how good we are!

Zero conditional

if clause	main clause
if/when + **present simple**	**main verb** + **present simple**
When I **meet** my sister	we often **talk** for hours.

We use the zero conditional to talk about something that always or usually happens.

*If/When she **sings**, everyone **stops** to listen.*
*I **don't watch** TV if/when I **have** work to do.*

First conditional

if clause	main clause
if + **present tense**	**will/could/might** + **infinitive**
If you **like** action,	you**'ll enjoy** this film.

We use the first conditional to talk about a possible action in the future.

*If you **don't understand** the words, you **could look** them up online.*
*You**'ll be** late for your meeting, if you **don't leave** now.*

Practice

1 **Complete the zero and first conditional sentences with the correct form of the verbs in brackets.**

a When she .... (see) her friends, they always .... (talk) about work.

b If you .... (meet) Callum today, you .... (be able) to tell him about the meeting next week.

c You .... (not get) any better if you .... (not practise).

d If Nick .... (call) me later, I .... (let) you know.

e When you .... (press) this key on the piano, it .... (make) a very deep sound.

f Dan .... (not come) to the play if it .... (start) in the afternoon.

g When he .... (not have to) go to work, he never .... (get up) early.

h If you .... (ask) her nicely, I'm sure she .... (help) you.

Second conditional

if clause	main clause
if + **past simple**	**would** + **infinitive**
If I **had** more free time,	I **would join** a drama club.

We use the second conditional:

• to talk about imaginary or unreal situations in the present.
  *If he **was** good, he**'d play** for a top team.*
  *My dog **would ask** me to feed him more often if he **could talk**!*

• to talk about present or future situations that are possible but unlikely.
  *If I **won** lots of money, I**'d buy** a sports car.*
  *If I **met** my favourite artist, I **would ask** her how she got where she is now.*

• to give advice.
  *If I **were** you, I**'d start** looking for a new job.*
  *I **would work** harder if I **were** you.*

Practice

1 **Make second conditional sentences.**

a if / she / not stay up / so late, she / not feel / tired in the morning

b if / I / have / his number, I / call / him

c if / she / be / good, / they / offer / her the job

d if / I / not have to / work, I / come / with you

e if / he / be / more careful, he / not make / so many mistakes

f if / you / lie / to me, I / be / very angry

Unless, in case, if I were you

Unless

We can use *unless* instead of *if not*.

*I can't help you **if** you **don't tell** me your problem.*
*I can't help you **unless** you **tell** me your problem.*
***If** he **doesn't get** that job, Sam won't be happy.*
***Unless** he **gets** that job, Sam won't be happy.*

Note: We don't use a negative verb after *unless*.

Unless you ~~don't invite~~ invite him, he won't come to the party.

In case

We can use *(just) in case* instead of *if* when we want to stress 'to be safe or prepared'.

*I'll take my coat **(just) in case** it gets cold.*
*I always have my phone **(just) in case** I need to call someone.*

If I were you

We can use *if I were you* to give someone advice. We use it in second conditional sentences.

***If I were you**, I would change football teams.*
*I'd take my coat **if I were you**. It's freezing outside!*

Practice

1 **Complete the sentences with *unless* or *in case*.**

a My friends won't come .... you want them to.

b We bought tickets early .... they sold out.

c I won't watch you, ... it makes you nervous.

d You won't survive in show business .... you have contacts.

e My little sister won't go on stage .... my mum goes with her.

f I'll stay with Robert, ... he needs my help.

Present simple passive

subject +	be (am/ is/are) +	+ past participle (+ by)	
The river	is	cleaned	every year.
The bottles	aren't	used	again.
The articles	are	written by the students.	

Past simple passive

subject +	be (was/ were) +	+ past participle (+ by)	
The trees	were	destroyed by the fire.	
The caves	were	found by a tourist.	
The book	was	published	in 2018.

We use the present simple passive or past simple passive:

- when we want to focus on the action more than the person that does or did the action.
  *The old clothes **are recycled**.*
  *The bridge **was repaired**.*

- when we don't know or don't want to say who does or did the action, or when it's obvious who did it.
  *The film **was watched** around the world.*
  *My phone **was stolen** at the train station.*

When we know or want to mention who does or did the action, we use *by*.

*The island was discovered **by a famous scientist**.*

Verbs without an object (e.g. *come, go, happen, arrive*) are not used in the passive because there is no object to become the subject.

Note: When you form the passive, make sure you use the correct form of *be*. To do this, look at the subject and think about whether it is singular or plural.

***The pizza was** delivered by someone on a bike.*
***Pizzas were** invented in Italy.*

Practice

1 Complete the sentences with the present simple or past simple passive form of these verbs.

> clean   collect   deliver   film   make
> play   prepare   speak   steal   waste

a English .... all around the world.

b These chocolates .... by hand in Switzerland last week.

c A parcel .... for you yesterday.

d The meals .... by professional chefs every day.

e Some jewellery .... from their house yesterday.

f The office .... every day by a team of cleaners.

g Tonnes of water .... every day when people leave taps running.

h A large amount of rubbish .... from the beach last week.

i The movie .... in a castle in Wales.

j Football .... in nearly every country in the world.

2 Complete the text with the correct active or passive form of the verbs in brackets.

Forest food

Last week I **(a)** .... (take) to an amazing restaurant for a friend's birthday. It's called The Green Forest Café and it **(b)** .... (locate) in a forest about thirty kilometres from my town. We drove to a car park nearby and then we **(c)** .... (walk) for about ten minutes through the trees to get to the café.

The building **(d)** .... (make) from wood. It has large windows and a glass ceiling, so you really feel part of the forest around you. The food is delicious. The salad and vegetables **(e)** .... (grow) locally and they **(f)** .... (freshly/pick) every day. We **(g)** .... (serve) our meal by a really friendly waiter, who **(h)** .... (explain) some of the things we could see around us. It was really interesting. We all enjoyed the experience a lot.

Have/Get something done

subject +	*have/ get +*	object +	past participle	
Present simple				
We	have	our pool	cleaned	every week.
I	get	my hair	cut	at Headlines.
Past simple				
She	had	her photo	taken	for her passport.
I	got	my teeth	checked	last week.

We use *have/get something done* when somebody else does something for us. We often pay them to do it for us. *Get something done* means the same as *have something done,* but it is less formal. We use it when we are talking.

I get my make-up done by Selina.

When we want to say who does the action for us, we use *by.*

He had his room decorated by a professional.

Practice

1 Complete the sentences with the present or past simple form of have/get something done.

a I .... (have; repair / my phone) yesterday.

b We .... (get; deliver / our post) every day at about 11 a.m.

c Louise .... (get; cut / her hair) last weekend.

d Tom .... (have; wash / his car) every week.

e They .... (have; clean / the offices) four times a week.

f My grandad .... (have; paint / this portrait) twenty years ago.

g I .... (get; fix / my camera) today.

h We .... (have; paint / the house) every two years.

Defining relative clauses

That's the girl	**who/that**	won first prize.
The train	**which/that**	leaves in ten minutes is full.
That's the place	**where**	we need to meet.
That's the man	**whose**	car was stolen.

We use defining relative clauses to describe exactly which people, things, places, etc. we mean. We use:

* *who* or *that* for people
* *which* or *that* for things/animals
* *where* for places
* *whose* to show possession.

Defining relative clauses can give us information about the subject or the object of the main clause. We often use them to join two sentences.
A girl found my passport. (*A girl* is the subject.)
She was very nice.
*The girl **who found** my passport was very nice.*
*I met **a man** yesterday.* (*A man* is the object.)
He speaks seven languages.
*The man **who I met** yesterday speaks seven languages.*

We can leave out the relative pronoun when it is the object of the relative clause.
*The man **I met** yesterday speaks seven languages.*

We don't use commas in defining relative clauses.

We use *whose* as the possessive form of *who*.
*This is Ella, **whose** family I travelled with last summer.*

Practice

1 **Choose the correct words to complete the sentences.**

a Is that the woman *which / who* interviewed you for the job?

b The singer *that / which* I like watching most on stage is Ed Sheeran.

c The performers *which / who* we saw at the festival were great.

d I'd like to find a flight *that / who* goes direct.

e Do you know the name of the song *which / where* is playing now?

f There are some beaches *where / who* it's dangerous to swim.

g That's the woman *which / who* I saw when at the station.

h The man *which / who* sat next to me on the train came from Turkey.

2 **Circle the relative pronoun if it is not necessary.**

a The hotel where we stayed was really expensive.

b The girl who I sat next to at school is famous now.

c The website which you recommended was really useful.

d We went to a restaurant where you had to cook your own food!

e He thanked the man who gave him directions.

f Is that the song which you said won the competition?

Modals of obligation, prohibition and necessity

Present

must	I **must get** *a new passport*.
	You **mustn't use** *a mobile phone on the plane*.
have to	We **have to collect** *the tickets from the station*.
	He **has to stay** here.
	They **don't have to leave** *now*.
	She **doesn't have to pay** for her ticket.
	Do we **have to go** now?
	Does he **have to be** here?

Past

had to	*I was late, so I* **had to run** *to the bus stop*.
	We **didn't have to walk** *because the bus came*.
	Did you **have to buy** another ticket?

Future

will have to	We**'ll have to go** *home soon*.
	You **won't have to talk** *to him again*.
	Will she **have to find** *a different flight?*

We use *must* when we think it is very important or necessary to do something.

*I **must buy** a new bag for the journey.*

We use *mustn't* when it's important or necessary not to do something or when something is prohibited.

*You **mustn't tell** him about the party.*

We use *have to* to talk about something that is important or necessary, often because it's a general rule.

*All passengers **have to show** their passports before they get on the plane.*

We use *don't have to* to talk about something that isn't necessary or when there is no obligation.

*You **don't have to sit** there if you don't want to.*

We use *had to* to talk about obligation in the past.

*I **had to buy** another ticket.*

We use *will have to* to talk about obligation in the future.

*You**'ll have to take** the bus to the airport.*

Need to

We use *need to/don't need to* when we think something is/isn't necessary but not an obligation.

*We **need to see** our friends before we leave.*

Practice

1   Choose the correct words to complete the sentences.

a   Men *have to / need to* wear a tie at the office. It's a rule.

b   We *mustn't / needn't* wear trainers. They're not allowed.

c   We *had to / must* hand in our report yesterday.

d   You *don't need to / mustn't* bring a camera. I've got one.

e   Next week we *will have to / must* give a presentation at work.

f   You *don't need to / mustn't* join the football team. It's up to you.

2   Complete the text below with the correct form of *have to*, *must* or *need to*.

My advice for a study tour

On our last study tour we went to Rome and I learnt a lot about travelling. Here's some helpful advice for what to do when you are on a study tour with your college.

- You **(a)** .... look after all your money. Ask the group leaders to hold it for you.

- Normally, you **(b)** .... allow for twenty euros a day but you don't **(c)** .... take more than this.

- At the airport you'll **(d)** .... collect your luggage and take it to check-in. Nobody will do it for you and the check-in staff **(e)** .... know it's your luggage.

- You **(f)** .... write you flight number down so you're sure you're in the right place at the right time.

- You **(g)** .... leave your luggage anywhere. Make sure it's always with you.

- You **(h)** .... keep your passport with you at all times. Put is somewhere safe. Make sure no one can take it.

Reported speech – statements

direct speech	reported speech
'I **take** photos of the stars.'	Liam said (that) he **took** photos of the stars.
'I **can** see it.'	Elena said (that) she **could** see it.
'I **will** do it again.'	Nathan said (that) he **would** do it again.

We use reported speech to tell somebody else what a person said.

*Liam said (that) he **read** about the stars every night.*

In reported speech, the main verb usually moves back one tense into the past.

*She said, 'I **want** to be a dancer.'*
*She said (that) she **wanted** to be a dancer.*

Practice

1   Rewrite the statements in reported speech.

a   'I love playing guitar,' said Mike.

    ....

b   'That's really interesting', said Jess.

    ....

c Lexi said, 'I'll call you later.'

....

d Ahmed said, 'I'm starting a new project.'

....

e 'I can't come to your party,' Rene told Sandra.

....

f 'The bus will leave soon,' Keira told Jake.

....

Reported speech – questions

Yes/No questions

direct speech	reported speech
She asked me, '**Are** you **studying** Arabic?'	She asked **if** I **was studying** Arabic.
She asked me, '**Do** you **live** in London?	She asked me **if** I **lived** in London.

When we report *yes/no* questions, the verb is not in question form and we don't use the auxiliary verb. We use *if* instead.

Wh- questions

direct speech	reported speech
She asked me, '**What's** your name?'	She asked me **what** my name **was**.'

When we report *wh-* questions, the verb is not in question form – we use the same structure as in statements. We repeat the question word in the reported question.

We use *say* or *tell* when reporting statements. *Tell* needs an object.

Adam said, 'I love photography.'
*Adam **said** (that) he loved photography.*
Lizzie told the receptionist, 'I need to collect a form.'
*Lizzie **told the receptionist** (that) she needed to collect a form.*

We use *ask* in reported questions. We can use it with or without an object.

'What happened?' he asked.
*He **asked** what had happened.*
'Where are you?' she asked me.
*She **asked me** where I was.*

Practice

2 Rewrite the reported questions as direct speech.

a Jamie asked me what I was cooking.

....

b Marie asked us if we had finished.

....

c Ian asked me what I would like.

....

d Marta asked us if we could help her.

....

e Zak asked me if I had seen Piotr.

....

f The tennis coach asked us what we wanted to do next.

....

Pronouns in reported speech

In reported speech, we change subject pronouns (*I, you, he, she*, etc.), possessive pronouns (*mine, yours, his, hers*, etc.) and possessive adjectives (*my, your, his, her*, etc.) so that it's clear who or what they refer to.
*Sandra said, '**My** hobby is painting.'*
*Sandra told me (that) **her** hobby was painting.*

Practice

3 Complete the sentences with the correct pronouns and possessive adjectives.

a 'You need to come back later,' the woman told him.

The woman said that .... needed to come back later.

b 'We need to leave,' said the man.

The man said that .... needed to leave.

c 'Your brother is my best friend,' David told me.

David said that .... brother was .... best friend.

d 'I've got your book,' my friend said to me.

My friend told .... that .... had .... book.

Indirect questions

Yes/No questions

direct question	indirect question
Is it a difficult job?	**Can you tell me if it's** a difficult job?
Do they live here?	**Do you know if they live** here?

Wh- questions

direct question	indirect question
Where do you practise?	Can you tell me where you practise?
Why do you enjoy your hobby?	Can I ask why you enjoy your hobby?

In indirect questions, we use the same verb form as in statements – the verb is not in question form.

In *yes/no* questions, we use *if*. In *wh-* questions we use the question word.

Does he work here?
Can you tell me if he works here?
What time does the concert start?
Do you know what time the concert starts?

Practice

1   **Choose the correct words to complete the sentences.**

   a   Fay asked *when / if* I was cold.

   b   Michiko asked *which / if* coat was mine.

   c   Lynn asked *what / if* I liked watching sport.

   d   Delia asked *what / if* I was having for dinner.

   e   Simon asked *where / if* I went at the weekend.

   f   James asked *where / if* I could help him.

Past perfect

Positive

I/You/He/She/It/We/They	'd (had)	finished.

Negative

I/You/He/She/It/We/They	hadn't (had not)	finished.

Questions

Had	I/you/he/she/it/we/they	finished?

Short answers

Yes,	I/you/he/she/it/we/they	had.
No,		hadn't.

We use the past perfect to talk about something that was completed at an earlier point in the past.

*I got a lovely surprise on my birthday. My colleagues **had organised** a party.*

Practice

1   **Find and correct the mistakes in six of the sentences.**

   a   I couldn't call him because I left my phone at home.

   b   After we'd finished lunch, we carried on shopping.

   c   I had stay up too late, so I couldn't get up early.

   d   I was hungry in the evening because I missed lunch.

   e   Theo's phone had no battery because he'd forgotten to charge it.

   f   Eleanor chose a film that we already seen.

   g   The library closed early because the heating break down.

   h   I couldn't read what I'd wrote in my notebook.

Past perfect and Past simple

We use the past perfect with the past simple to show that one action happened before another in the past. The past perfect simple describes the action that happened first and the past simple describes the action that happened second.

past ————✕————————✕———— now
         The meeting   *when Ben*
         had finished   ***arrived***.

(First, the meeting finished. Then, Ben arrived.)

We can also say:
*When Ben **arrived**, the meeting **had finished**.*

We use many of the same time expressions that we use with the present perfect. We use adverbs of time, e.g. *already*, *ever*, *just* and *never*.

*She offered us a snack but we'd **just** had lunch.*

*Mark was funny. I'd **never** met anyone quite like him. I didn't want any more surprises. I'd **already** had enough!*

We use time linkers (e.g. *after*, *before*, *by*, *once*, *until*, *when*) to talk about two actions in the same sentence.

***After** they had seen the concert, they went to bed.*
***By the time** we got to the station, the train had left.*
***Once** it stopped raining, we went for a walk.*
*Emily had left for work **when** I got up.*

Practice

1 **Complete the text with the past simple or past perfect form of the verbs in brackets.**

A bad start to the day

Bethan decided to take the bus to the office. Her car **(a)** .... (break down) the day before, so she couldn't drive.

She **(b)** .... (just/get) there when the bus arrived. She got on and **(c)** .... (reach) into her bag to get her purse. That was when she realised she **(d)** .... (leave) it at home.

Walking was her only option but it was raining and she **(e)** .... (not/bring) an umbrella. Still, she started to walk. After a few minutes, a car **(f)** .... (drive) past her really fast and **(g)** .... (hit) a huge puddle. The water **(h)** .... (fly) up in the air and **(i)** .... (land) on Bethan. She looked like she **(j)** .... (just/get) out of the bath!

Used to

Positive

I/You/He/She/It/We/They	**used to**	**collect** comics.

Negative

I/You/He/She/It/We/They/	**didn't use to**	**have** any hobbies.

Questions

Did	I/you/he/she/it/ we/ they	**use to**	**have** any hobbies?

We use *used to* to talk about something that happened regularly in the past, but does not happen now. We use it to refer to past habits or states.

*He **used to enjoy** drama at school, but he doesn't do it now.*
*I **didn't use to watch** horror films, but I like them now.*
*You speak French well. **Did** you **use to live** in France?*

We often use *used to* with *never*.

*I **never used to like** curry but I do now.*
*Jack **never used to be** so shy.*

We don't use *used to*:

- to talk about an action which happened only once or twice
- with a time expression that tells us how many times an action happened
- with a time expression that tells us when an action happened.

*I used to visit **visited** India a few times when I was young.*
*We used to go **went** swimming last August.*

We don't use *used to* to say how long a **state** lasted. But we can use it to talk about how long a repeated or regular past **action** lasted.

*They used to live **lived** here for ten years.*
*I used to like **liked** this song for about two years but I don't now.*
*We **used to play** in the tree house for hours.*
*She **used to practise** singing for two hours a day.*

Practice

1 **Complete the sentences with the correct form of *used to*.**

a I .... (not) like running but I love it now.

b .... (you) go to the cinema often when you were young?

c Ksenja .... read comics but now she reads novels.

d .... (you) live with your grandparents?

e Amanda .... work abroad every summer but she doesn't now.

f .... (your sister) have curly hair?

g Jacob .... (not) say much in meetings but he's much chattier these days.

h I .... (not) be interested in science but now I quite like it.

Part 1 Phases 1 and 2

In Phase 1 of Part 1, you answer simple questions about your name, your age, where you live and who you live with. In Phase 2 you answer one or two more questions on personal topics, such as your hobbies, home life, daily routine, likes and dislikes, and so on.

Exam help

- Phase 1 questions are always the same. Practise answering them clearly and confidently.
- You only need to give short answers in Phase 1.
- Give longer answers in Phase 2. Explain and give reasons for your answer.
- Some questions begin with the words 'Tell us about …'. Say as much as you can about the topic.
- Think about the tense: the question may be about the present, the past or the future.
- If you don't understand a question, ask the examiner to repeat it.

Useful language

Introducing yourself
My name's/I'm …
My friends call me …

Giving personal information
I'm … years old.
I live in the city centre/a small village.
I come from a small/large family.
I'm an only child.
I've got an older brother and two younger sisters.
I live with (my parents).
I'm studying chemical engineering.
I'm training to be a train driver.
I'm a teacher.

Likes and dislikes
I like/love/prefer …
The … I like best is …
My favourite … is …
I'm (not) (very) keen on/fond of …
I don't like …
I (don't) really enjoy …
I'd rather … than …
What I like about … is …
I don't mind …

Practice Part 1

1 **Look at these things students said in their exam. Complete the sentences with the words from the box.**

about	at	do	got	have	near
takes	when				

a I've .... two older sisters.

b I'm training to be an architect, but it .... a long time.

c I'm studying modern languages .... university.

d I .... to get up very early in the morning because it's a long way to my school.

e Our flat's in the old part of the city, ... the main square.

f I hope to work in marketing in the future, and I think I'll need English to .... that.

g Although I don't have very much spare time, I go cycling .... I can.

h I go to college by bus every day and it takes .... half an hour.

2 **Add a reason or explanation to complete the sentences. Use a verb and the words from the box or your own ideas.**

clever lyrics	cold weather
get on well/sisters	Italian food
videos and podcasts	with a team

a I love pasta because …

b I'm not keen on skiing because …

c I like spending time at home because …

d What I like about football is …

e I don't like studying from books – I'd rather …

f My favourite music is rap because …

In this part of the test, you speak on your own for about one minute. You describe a photograph. Remember that your photograph is on a different topic from your partner's.

Exam help

- ✓ Begin by talking about the general situation, then talk about the people.
- ✓ Use the present tense to talk about what you can see.
- ✓ Talk about the people, their appearance, clothes, feelings and so on.
- ✓ Use the present continuous to talk about what people are doing.
- ✓ Talk about the objects, the weather, the things you see in the background.
- ✓ Use your own ideas about the photograph and say why you think that.
- ✓ Use other words to say what you want or move on to a different part of the photo.

Useful language

Talking about the photograph

In the foreground/background/middle, there are/I can see some …
At the back/front/top/bottom I can see …
On the left/right there's a/an …

Talking about the people

She's (quite/rather) short/tall.
He's got dark/short/straight hair.
He's wearing jeans and a strange hat.
He looks about … years old.

Talking about what the people are doing

They're indoors/outdoors.
She's sitting on a train/bus.
They're at a swimming pool/in a big room.
He seems to be in the mountains/by the sea.
They're eating breakfast in a hotel/café.

Talking about the place

It's a nice room with large windows.
The (square) looks very crowded.
It seems to be a very old bridge.
It's very sunny at the beach.

Giving your own ideas

They seem rather sad/quite happy/a bit bored to me.
It looks as if they're having fun/problems because …
Something must be funny because they're laughing.
I'm not sure, but I think it might be in China because of the buildings.
I don't know what this is, but I guess it's a …
I suppose they could be friends or sisters.
He's probably a famous person because everyone's looking at him.

When you're not sure of a word

I don't know the word in English, but you … with it.
It looks like a …, but it's bigger.
It's a thing/device you use to …
I don't know what it's called but you keep … in it.
It's the place where you …

Practice Part 2

1 Choose the correct words to complete the sentences.

a He might be rich – he's wearing very smart *clothes / dress*.

b Maybe they're on holiday because they *seem / must* very relaxed.

c She's winning the race because the other runners are a long way *before / behind* her.

d They could *come / take* from the same family.

e I think he's worried *because / when* he's going to miss his flight.

f When I *watch / see* the cake, it makes me think it's someone's birthday.

g He's *probable / probably* the girl's brother because he looks a lot like her.

h The woman looks a bit worried *to / of* me.

2 What is each student describing? Choose the correct word from the box for each sentence.

| cash desk   helmet   kettle   necklace |
| oven   remote control |

a It's a device you use to change the channel on the TV. ....

b It's a pretty thing you wear round your neck. ....

c It's the thing in the kitchen you use to bake bread and cakes. ....

d You use one for boiling water when you make hot drinks. ....

e It's the place where you pay for something in a shop. ....

f You wear one on your head when you go cycling. ....

In this part of the test, you discuss a task with your partner. You can start by talking about the different options in turn, and responding to each other's comments.

Exam help

- ✔ Listen carefully to the instructions.
- ✔ The examiner describes the situation and tells you and your partner what to discuss.
- ✔ If you're not sure what to do, ask the examiner to repeat the task.
- ✔ Look at the page of pictures. The picture in the middle tells you the situation.
- ✔ The task has a title to help you remember what to talk about.
- ✔ Remember, you have to talk to your partner in this part. The examiner just listens to your conversation.

Useful language

Getting started
Where shall we start/begin?
Let's start with this one. Is this a good … ?

Asking for opinions
What do you think of this idea?
I'm not sure about … What do you think?
Do you think … would be a good idea for them?
What about … ?

Explaining opinions
I think a … is a good prize because …
In my opinion, … is a good idea because …
I think they should buy … because …
I don't think … is a good idea because …

Agreeing
I agree.
That's true/right/what I think, too.
That's a good point.
Exactly!

Disagreeing
Maybe that's not such a good idea because …
I'm not sure about that because …
I don't agree with you really because …
Sorry, I don't think so.

Moving on
Let's talk about this activity next.
OK, but what about … ?
So, which one do you think is best?
What shall we choose then?
Let's choose the …

Practice Part 3

1 **Two students are discussing a Part 3 task. What is student B doing in each conversation? Write the correct letter: A agreeing, D disagreeing, O giving an opinion, R giving a reason, or T changing the topic?**

a A: I think a box of chocolates would be a good prize.

   B: Really? I'm not sure about that. ……..

b A: Why do you think a teddy bear is a good gift for the teacher?

   B: Because everybody likes teddy bears. ……..

c A: What do you think about the family having a barbecue in the garden?

   B: I think that could be a good idea if the weather is good. ……..

d A: Why don't you like the idea of the girl going to the cinema?

   B: Because it's not a good way to make new friends – you can't talk to people there. ……..

e A: If the family go sightseeing in the city, they can talk about it afterwards.

   B: I see what you mean – that's true. ……..

f A: What about ice-skating?

   B: Yes, the whole family would enjoy that. ……..

g A: The T-shirt's a very useful present for the friends to give the girl.

   B: Possibly. Let's talk about some of the other things before we decide, though. ……..

h A: So do we both think the camera is a good gift?

   B: I think so – it seems a nice idea. ……..

2 **Put the words in the correct order to make sentences from Part 3 discussions.**

a start / this / with / let's / activity

b do / this / what / think / you / idea / of?

c what / that's / think / I / too

d I / agree / we're / think / going / to / don't / that / about / idea!

e that's / I'm / good / not / a / activity / young / for / children / sure

f I / that's / don't / I / because / think / don't / very / agree / useful

g point / a / that's / good

h will / do / which / activity / you / the / family / all / think / enjoy?

i the / choose / why / we / don't / hat?

j choose / so / box / the / chocolates / of / let's

In this part of the test, the examiner asks you questions about the topic of Part 3.

Exam help

- ✓ The questions are on the same topic as Part 3, but the questions are more general, they're not about that situation.
- ✓ Talk about your own personal experiences and opinions.
- ✓ The examiner may ask a question to you directly, or may ask a question for either of you to answer.
- ✓ Listen to what your partner says because the examiner may ask you if you agree, or ask what you think about the same question.

Useful language

Giving yourself time to think

That's a difficult question – let me think for a moment.

Sorry, I don't understand. Could you say that again, please?

Sorry, I've forgotten the question. Could you repeat it, please?

Giving personal opinions

For me, the most important thing is …

In my opinion, the most interesting … is/ are …

If you ask me, the best thing is …

I think the main reason for … is to …

Giving examples

For example, …

Let me give you an example, …

I think a good example of that is when …

Agreeing and disagreeing with what your partner says

I agree with … when he/she says … because

That's what I think, too, because …

I partly agree with that idea, but …

I don't agree with that really because …

To be honest, I'm not sure about that because …

Practice Part 4

1   **Match the students' answers (A–F) to a reason (i–vi).**

   A   If you ask me, it's important to do homework because …

   B   In my opinion, it's much nicer to relax on a beach when you're on holiday, although …

   C   I prefer watching sport to doing it …

   D   People need to stay healthy but they don't need to do sport – for example, …

   E   Well, I don't like big cities, so …

   F   I don't do anything with my friends at the end of the day because …

   i   if I could choose, I would live in a small town or village.

   ii   I'm usually at home with my family.

   iii   you can learn more about what you've done in your lessons.

   iv   I know some people like skiing, so they prefer cold places.

   v   I'm not very good at team sports!

   vi   they could just eat healthy food.

2   **Now match the examiner's questions to the students' answers in Exercise 1. There is one extra answer you don't need to use.**

   a   Do you prefer going on holiday in hot or cold places?

   b   Is it a good idea for everyone to do a sport?

   c   What do you usually do in the evenings with friends?

   d   Do you think everyone should do homework every day?

   e   Is it better to live in a city or a small town?

3   **Complete the students' answers with the words and phrases from the box.**

honest	in fact	let me	moment
opinion	rather	repeat	seems

   a   Well, I'd _____ play a sport like football than tennis because I love taking part in team games.

   b   In my _____ the school day is too long and the holidays are too short! I like having a lot of free time in the summer.

   c   I hate doing homework – _____ , I think we have to do too much! I usually spend two hours doing it every evening.

   d   To be _____ , I don't like reading books very much, but I do sometimes read a book after I've seen the film.

   e   I think live music is great – _____ tell you about the last concert I went to.

   f   It _____ to me that it's important to eat healthy food, as well as doing exercise, if you want to keep fit.

   g   Sorry, I didn't understand. Could you _____ the question, please?

   h   I need to think about that for a _____ – it's a difficult question.

WRITING BANK

Part 1: Email

In this part of the test, you have to reply to an email that has been sent to you. You do this using four notes written next to the email.

Sample answer

See Test 1, Writing Part 1, question 1 on page 25.

New Message

This is about the first note.	Hi Anna,
	Winning the competition was a wonderful surprise! I've always wanted to go on a photography holiday.
This is about the second note and gives reasons for the choice.	Thank you for giving me the opportunity to learn from a professional photographer. Taking good pictures of the natural world is a real challenge, so I'd like to go to the mountains. I live in a big city, so that option is less interesting for me.
This is about the third note, with reasons.	I'd like my cousin and my mother to come, too, as they've always wanted to improve their photography skills. I'd love to know where we'll be going and how we
This is about the fourth note.	will get there.
The email ends in a polite and friendly way.	Thanks again and best wishes,
	Helena

Exam help

✓ Read the email carefully.
✓ Read the notes one by one and for each note, underline the important words in the email. Underlining the key words will remind you that you must use all the notes, and which part of the email the note refers to.
✓ Start with a friendly, informal greeting (*Hi Anna,*).
✓ Write complete sentences and check that you are using the correct form of verbs (present, past or future).
✓ Don't be afraid to use some interesting vocabulary and expressions you know.
✓ Make sure you write about 100 words. Try not to write fewer than 90.

Useful language

Starting the email

How are you?
I hope you and your family are well.
It was great to hear from you.
I'm really looking forward to your visit.
I'm excited about our trip too.
… was a wonderful surprise!

Saying thank you

Thank you for giving me the opportunity to …
Thank you so much for …
That's very kind of you.
Thanks again (for …)

Explaining or giving reasons

Taking good pictures is a real challenge, so …
I live in a big city, so…
… as they've always wanted to improve their photography skills.
That would be lovely because I've never been there before.

Making a suggestion

Maybe we can …
Why don't we … ?
How about … ?
I think it would be a good idea to …
I think we should …
Let's …

Asking for more information

I'd love to know where we'll be going first.
I wonder how we will get there.
What clothes should I bring?
Who's coming with us?
What time do you plan to leave?

Finishing a message

Have a great weekend!
Write soon!
Let me know what you think!
See you next week!
Love,
Best wishes,

Practice Part 1: Email

1 Find and correct twelve mistakes in the email. Think about grammar, spelling and using the correct words.

New Message

Hi Anna,

Thank you for your email. It was really nice surprise. I never expected to winning the competision!

Going on a photography holiday is very exiting. I rather go to big city because is more fun and I really like take photos of people. The mountains could be a bit bored for me.

I'd like my cousin and best friend to coming with me as they are also very keen with photography.

I just have one question: when is the holiday start?

Best wishes,

Jan

2 Complete the sentences with the linking words from the box.

because but if so when

a I'm a vegetarian, ... I don't eat beef.

b I'd like to go for a swim .... you'd enjoy that too.

c I'll send you a message .... I get to the station.

d I wrote to my friend .... she didn't reply.

e I bought this tennis racket .... it was quite cheap.

3 Add reasons to complete the sentences. Use a different reason for each sentence.

a I can't go to the cinema this evening because …

b I love playing badminton because …

c I don't often eat meat because …

d I see my cousins every week because …

e I don't like camping because …

f I enjoy playing computer games because …

Planning your answer

Aim to write several paragraphs, not just one long paragraph. Don't forget to start with a greeting.

Paragraph 1

Start this paragraph with an introductory sentence (for example, *How are you? It was great to hear from you*). Then include what the first note tells you to write.

Paragraphs 2 – 3/4

These should deal with the other three notes. If you don't have much to write for one of the notes, you can include what you need to write for two of the notes in a single paragraph. Avoid paragraphs of only one sentence.

Finishing your email

Don't forget to add a comment (for example, *Thanks again! See you soon*) and a way of saying goodbye (for example, *Love, Best wishes*) at the end and put your name at the bottom.

How to use the written notes

Each note will usually only be one or two words long. Decide what kind of information you need to include for each one (for example, a reason, a suggestion, saying thank you), then think of what you could say.

Make sure you include as much information as you can, for example, when you have to explain or give reasons. Very short answers will not get good marks!

Make sure you deal with all four notes. You will lose marks if you don't, so tick them off as you write your email. Check carefully that you have done what each of the four notes asks you to.

Checklist

When you finish writing a short message, use this checklist:

Content
Have you dealt with all four notes?

Communicative achievement
Who are you writing to? A friend or someone you don't know? Have you used a suitable style?

Organisation
Have you divided your email into paragraphs, with a suitable greeting and way of saying goodbye?
Have you put your name at the bottom?

Language
Have you used the correct tenses?
Have you used a range of vocabulary?
Have you checked your spelling?

In this part of the test, you can choose to write an article about a topic. You do this using some questions that are presented in an announcement on an English-language website or in an English-language magazine.

Sample answer

See Test 1, Writing Part 2, question 2 on page 27.

Use the title that is in the task or make up your own title.

One way of starting your article is with a question, which you can then answer.

This answers the first question, about the kind of films you like.

Words like 'although' help you to organise your ideas.

Don't be afraid to give your opinions.

This answers the second question, 'Why?', giving reasons why you like horror films.

This paragraph answers the third question, about where you prefer watching films.

Horror films!

Do you agree that horror films are the best thing ever? Some people can't stand them, but I just think they're really brilliant. Although some of them are quite silly, others are made in a very clever way and I think the stories are unusual and exciting.

Sometimes it's fun to watch them at the cinema, with lots of people sitting terrified in the dark. But what I like best of all is watching a classic horror film at home with a couple of friends, so we can scream and shout as loud as we like. And we can make our own popcorn, too!

Useful language

Starting the article
Do you think that … ?
Have you ever thought about … ?
Do you agree that … ?
In my country/town/area, people …

Giving your opinion
I think …
I believe …
In my opinion, …

Comparing
… is more interesting/difficult/
popular than …
The most challenging/successful/
exciting … is …

Explaining or giving reasons
This is because …
That's why …
For this reason, …

Adding information
Also, …
In addition to this, …

Imagining things
What would happen if … ?
It would be fantastic/amazing/
interesting if …
People could try …
I wonder if …

Finishing your article
What do you think?
And …, too!

Exam help

- ✓ Read the task very carefully.
- ✓ In this task, you are going to write about films. There are two parts. The first part is about the kind of film you like best, and the second is about where you prefer to watch films. You must also explain your opinions.
- ✓ Underline the sentences in the sample answer that answer the first part of the question.
- ✓ Underline the sentences in the sample answer that answer the second part of the question.
- ✓ Write down some of your own opinions for each of the two parts, then think of the reasons for your opinions.
- ✓ Try to enjoy writing the article and remember, your readers should enjoy it too!
- ✓ When you've finished, make sure you've written about 100 words and check your article for spelling or grammar mistakes.

1 **Discuss the question in pairs. Talk about all the points.**

> A magazine has lots of articles. Some look interesting, some don't. What makes you want to start reading one of the articles?

Interesting information?   Good title?
Seems fun to read?   Interesting first line?

2 **You can make an article more interesting by starting with a question. Match the article titles (a–c) with the questions (i–v). There are two extra questions you do not need to use.**

   a   Making new friends

   b   The importance of friends

   c   How to help a good friend

   i   Do we really need friends in our lives?

   ii   Should we tell our new friends all our secrets?

   iii   How can we make new friends?

   iv   How do we communicate with our friends?

   v   What can we do when a friend needs us?

3 **You can make an article more interesting by giving personal opinions. Add your opinions to complete the sentences below.**

   a   You may not agree with me if I say that romantic films are …

   b   I'm sure that lots of people prefer films that teach them something, for example …

   c   Cinemas are not only places to see films, but also places where …

   d   Many young people are very sociable, so they like …

   e   Would you be surprised if I told you that my favourite films are … ?

Planning your answer

Different article tasks have different numbers of questions, but you should always be able to write a good answer in about 100 words.

Aim to write two or three paragraphs, not just one long paragraph.

Paragraph 1

You can use a question at the beginning if you want, and then answer it in the next sentence or sentences. This paragraph will introduce the main topic of the article. It may contain the answer to the first question in the task, but this depends on the task.

Paragraphs 2/3

This/These should contain your answers to the other questions that are asked in the task. Remember to give reasons as well as your opinion. Each paragraph should be several sentences long, and never just contain one sentence.

Checklist

When you finish writing a short message, use this checklist:

Content
Have you answered all of the questions in the task?
Have you added reasons to your opinions?

Communicative achievement
The article is for readers of a magazine or a website who you don't know, so have you used a suitable semi-formal style?

Organisation
Have you divided your article into paragraphs?
Have you organised your ideas in a logical way?

Language
Have you used the correct tenses?
Have you used a range of vocabulary?
Have you checked your spelling?

WRITING BANK

Part 2: Story

In this part of the test, you can choose to write a story. You are given the first sentence of the story and you have to continue the story for about 100 words.

Sample answer

See Test 1, Writing Part 2, question 3 on page 27.

Copy the first sentence from the task so it is the beginning of your story.	I was glad when my phone started to ring. I'd waited all day for Paul to call me and tell me if he'd passed his driving test. I hadn't wanted to ring him or message him to ask because he'd been very nervous about it.
Use the past perfect to talk about things that happened before the beginning of the story.	
Use linking words such as 'because' to connect your ideas.	But when I looked at my phone, it wasn't Paul calling. It was someone I didn't know. A strange voice said, 'Hi, I'm Paul's brother, look out of the window!' I saw a small car parked in the street, so I ran outside and there was Paul, sitting in the driver's seat, looking very pleased with himself. 'Come for a ride in my brother's car!' he said.
It's a good idea to write some longer sentences using linking words.	
You can describe what people looked like, or the way they were feeling, to make your story more interesting.	

Useful language

In a story,

- You need verbs in the past tense (for example, *were, ran, saw, kicked*) because the story happened in the past.
- You may need to use the past perfect to talk about things that happened before the beginning of the story.
- You may need to use the past continuous to talk about things happening at the same time as events in your story.
- You need to use words that link the actions in the past (for example, *after that, later, when*) to make your story easy to follow.
- You need to use a variety of adjectives and adverbs (for example, *exciting, frightened, scared, surprised, suddenly, amazingly*) to add interest and excitement to your story.
- Try to use words which mean the same (synonyms) instead of repeating the same word (for example, *nice* → *lovely* → *beautiful*).

Exam help

- ✓ Do not change the first sentence of the story.
- ✓ If the sentence is about a person, make sure your story is all about him/her.
- ✓ Divide your story into paragraphs so that it is easy to read.
- ✓ Make your story interesting by using a range of vocabulary.
- ✓ Make sure you write about 100 words. Try not to write fewer than 90.
- ✓ Check your grammar, particularly all your verb tenses.
- ✓ As well as telling the events of the story, you can add in what the people were thinking and/or what they said.

Practice Part 2: Story

1 Complete the story with the words from the box.

> dangerous   decided   didn't have
> had left   said   sat   scared   stupid
> suddenly   took   walked   was
> was playing   were

It was getting late, so Peter **(1)** .... to go home. He **(2)** .... goodbye to his friend and **(3)** .... to the bus stop. There **(4)** .... only a few other people in the street because it **(5)** .... almost eleven o'clock in the evening, but he wasn't **(6)** .... The town wasn't a **(7)** .... place. But he did feel that something wasn't quite right. He just couldn't say what it was exactly.

Peter **(8)** .... down to wait for the bus and **(9)** .... his phone out of his back pocket. He **(10)** .... his favourite game when **(11)** ...., he realised that he **(12)** .... his rucksack with him. He **(13)** .... it at his friend's house! Now he knew what was wrong, and he felt really **(14)** .... !

2 How did they feel? Complete the sentences with the adjectives from the box.

> confident   confused   delighted
> disappointed   frightened   shocked

a   Tom felt so .... that he couldn't move. He was terrified of spiders.

b   Sally felt very .... that she would win the tennis match.

c   What's the answer to this question? I'm really ....

d   Clare was .... when she heard her friend wouldn't be able to come to her party.

e   Simon was .... to see his old friend after so many years.

f   Clare was .... to hear that Mark had had an accident.

3 Write the first sentence of a story. Then follow these steps.

a   Give your sentence to a partner and look at the sentence that they give you.

b   Think up a story that continues this first sentence and make some notes about it.

c   Take turns to tell each other your story.

Planning your answer

Aim to write several paragraphs, not just one long paragraph.

Paragraph 1
Make sure that you have at least one more sentence in the first paragraph after the sentence given in the task.

Paragraph 2
This should contain any background information you need to give (for example, about the people or the place) and the first part of the story.

Paragraph 3
This should contain part of the story. Remember to add details to your story. This should mean that each paragraph is several sentences, not just one.

Paragraphs 4
If you choose to use four paragraphs, this should contain the final part of the story and a suitable sentence or sentences to finish the story in an entertaining way.

Checklist

When you finish writing a short message, use this checklist:

Content
Does your story have a beginning, middle and end?
Have you added details and language to make the story more interesting to read?

Communicative achievement
The story is for people who are reading for pleasure, so have you used a suitable entertaining style?

Organisation
Have you divided your story into paragraphs?
Have you included suitable linking words and phrases to join the parts of your story together?

Language
Have you used the correct tenses?
Have you used a range of vocabulary?
Have you checked your spelling?

Part 2 Candidate A

Photograph 1A

Photograph 2A

Photograph 3A

Photograph 4A

Part 2 Candidate A

Photograph 5A

Photograph 6A

Photograph 7A

Photograph 8A

TEST
1–2

VISUALS FOR SPEAKING TESTS

Photograph 1B

Photograph 2B

Photograph 3B

Photograph 4B

Part 2 Candidate B

Photograph 5B

Photograph 6B

Photograph 7B

Photograph 8B

Presents the people could buy for their friend

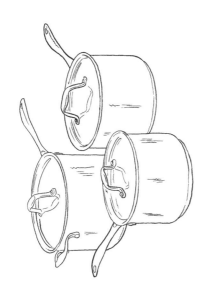

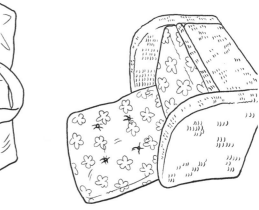

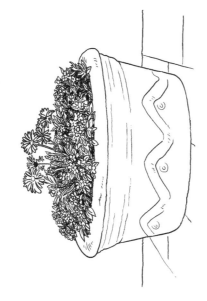

Things the school could buy to help its students

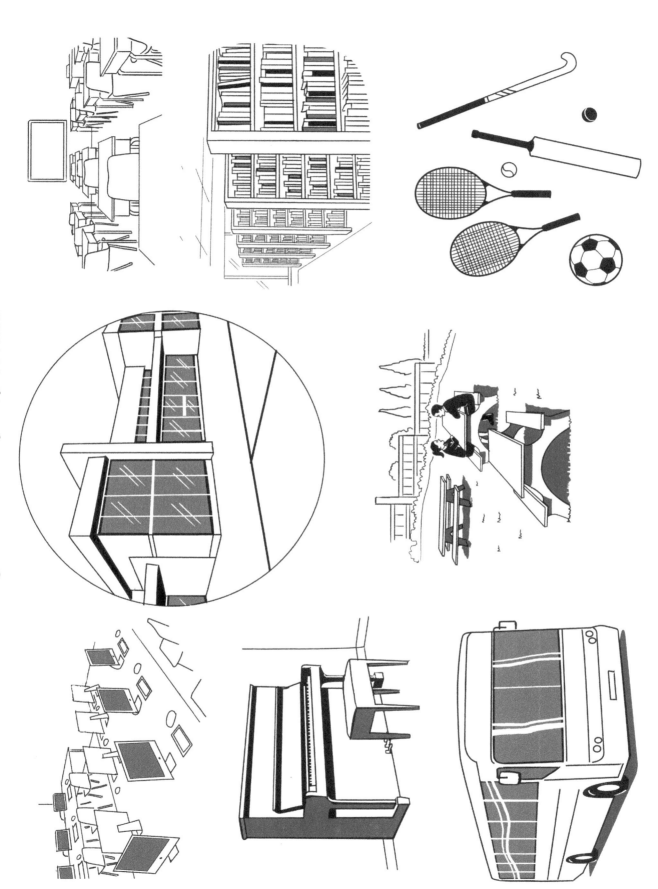

Presents the friends could buy for the woman

Things the family could do together

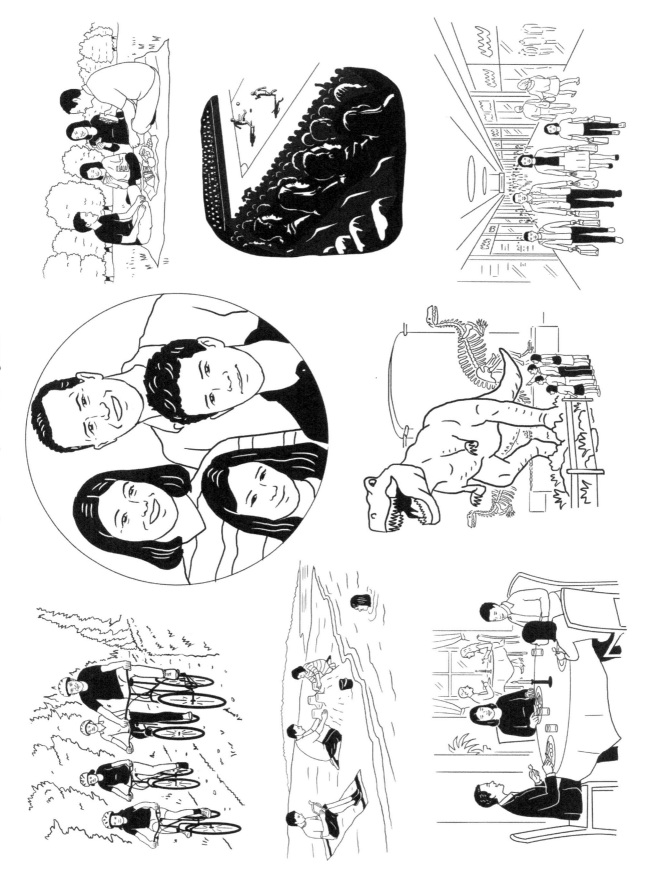

Things the two friends could do during the flight

Jobs the students could do during their holiday

Presents the children could buy their parents for their anniversary

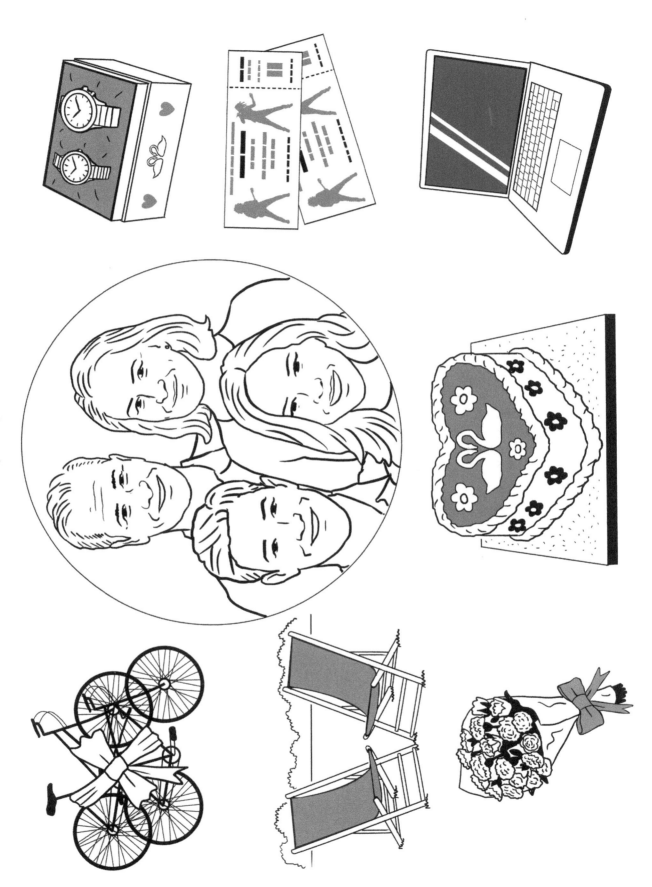

Places the family could go on holiday

1 How many marks are needed to pass the exam?
➤ To pass the exam with a grade C, you need around 60 percent of the total marks.

2 Do I have to pass each paper in order to pass the exam?
➤ No. Each paper doesn't have a pass or fail mark. Your overall grade comes from adding your marks on all four papers together

3 Are marks taken off for wrong answers?
➤ No. This means that, if you're not sure, you should always try to guess – you might be right.

4 Am I allowed to use a dictionary in the exam?
➤ No, this is not allowed during the exam.

5 In Writing Part 1 what happens if I don't write about all the points listed?
➤ You should write about all the things the task requires. The examiners are looking to see if you can provide the right information and good language.

6 In Writing Parts 1 and 2, what happens if I write too few or too many words?
➤ The word count is an important guide. It tells you how much to write to complete the task. But don't waste time counting every word – just make sure you use about the right number.

7 Generally, in the exam, if I'm not sure about an answer, can I give two possible answers?
➤ No. If there are two answers, and one of them is wrong, you will not get a mark. So you must decide on one answer to give.

8 In Writing Part 1, do contractions count as one word or two?
➤ Two. For example, mustn't = must + not = two words.

9 What happens if I make a spelling mistake in the Writing Parts?
➤ Spelling is one of several things the examiner considers when deciding what mark to give you. Check your spelling as much as possible.

10 What happens if I make a spelling mistake in Listening Part 3?
➤ It depends. If the examiner can still easily understand what word you meant to write, you will get the mark.

11 How many times will I hear each recording in the Listening paper?
➤ You will hear each recording twice.

12 In Listening Part 3, should I use the words I hear in the recording or is it better to use different words?
➤ You must write only words (or numbers) that you actually hear in the recording. Also, you must not change these words.

13 In Listening Part 3, what happens if my answer is too long to fit in the space on the answer sheet?
➤ Most answers are one or two words or a number. These answers will easily fit in the spaces on the answer sheet. If your answer is longer than this, it is probably either wrong, or you are including too much.

14 In the Speaking Test, can I take the test alone? Or can I choose my partner?
➤ You must take the Speaking Test with a partner. This is because your ability to discuss things with another student is an important part of what is tested.

15 For the Speaking Test, is it a good idea to prepare what I'm going to say in Part 1?
➤ It is, of course, good to prepare well for the exam. But you cannot know exactly what the examiner will ask beforehand, so you must listen very carefully to the examiner, and make sure you answer the questions relevantly.

16 In the Speaking Test, what if my partner makes a lot of mistakes, or doesn't talk much or talks too much?
➤ Don't worry about these things. The examiner will make sure you have a fair chance in every situation.